GROUP OF BIRCH TREES, WHITE EARTH, MINN.

HOW INDIANS USE WILD PLANTS

FOR FOOD, MEDICINE
AND CRAFTS

(formerly titled *Uses of Plants by the Chippewa Indians*)

Frances
Densmore

DOVER PUBLICATIONS, INC.
NEW YORK

NOTE ON THE PAGINATION

The page and plate reference numbers in this
edition conform to those of the original publication of this article in the *Forty-fourth Annual
Report of the Bureau of American Ethnology*.
Pages 1 through 274 of that *Report* were devoted
to entirely different subjects and were not written
by Miss Densmore. Her article is complete in this
volume.

This Dover edition, first published in 1974, is an unabridged
republication of an Accompanying Paper, "Uses of Plants by
the Chippewa Indians," (pages 275-397) in the *Forty-fourth
Annual Report of the Bureau of American Ethnology to the
Secretary of the Smithsonian Institution, 1926-1927*, as originally
published by the United States Government Printing Office,
Washington, in 1928.

International Standard Book Number: 0-486-23019-8
Library of Congress Catalog Card Number: 73-92500

Manufactured in the United States of America
Dover Publications, Inc., 31 East 2nd Street, Mineola, N.Y. 11501

CONTENTS

ILLUSTRATIONS

FOREWORD

The varied uses of plants by the Chippewa indicate the large extent to which they understood and utilized the natural resources of their environment. The present study is related, in two of its phases, to the study of Chippewa music which preceded it.[1] Herbs were used in the treatment of the sick and in the working of charms, and songs were sung to make the treatment and the charms effective. Songs of these classes having been recorded, the Indians were willing to bring specimens of the herbs and to explain the manner of their use. A majority of the informants on this subject were women and they became interested in describing the former methods of preparing vegetable foods. Both men and women related the uses of plants in medicine, economic life, and the useful and decorative arts. Plants and data were obtained on the White Earth, Red Lake, Cass Lake, Leech Lake, and Mille Lac Reservations in Minnesota, the Lac Court Oreilles Reservation in Wisconsin, and the Manitou Rapids Reserve in Ontario, Canada, the work continuing until 1925.

The writer gratefully acknowledges the assistance of those who have contributed to the result of the present undertaking. The specimens of plants were identified and their common names supplied by Mr. Paul C. Standley, of the United States National Museum. The reports on the recognized medicinal properties of the plants used by the Chippewa and on their active medical constituents were prepared by Dr. W. W. Stockberger, physiologist in charge of drug, poisonous, and oil plant investigations, Bureau of Plant Industry, United States Department of Agriculture, and valuable assistance in the classification of diseases and injuries treated by the Chippewa was given by Dr. D. S. Lamb, who at the time was pathologist at the Army Medical Museum, Washington, D. C. Assistance has also been received from members of the staff of the Bureau of American Ethnology and the United States National Museum in their special fields of research.

The work on the Manitou Rapids Reserve in Ontario was made possible by the courtesy of John P. Wright, Indian agent of the Canadian Government at Fort Frances, Ontario.

The collection of the material herewith presented would have been impossible without the cooperation of members of the Chippewa tribe. Their assistance is gratefully acknowledged, especially that of the principal interpreter, Mrs. Mary Warren English, of White Earth, Minn., which began in 1907 and continued about 15 years.

FRANCES DENSMORE.

---

[1] Chippewa Music, Bull. 45, 1910, and Chippewa Music II, Bull. 53, Bur. Amer. Ethn., 1013.

INFORMANTS [1]

Mrs. Mary Razer_____ Papa'gine'. (Grasshopper.)

Mrs. Louisa Martin_____ A'jawac'. (Wafted across.)

No'dinĕns'_____ Little wind.

Gage'wĭn[2]_____ Everlasting mist.

Mrs. Gage'wĭn _____ Nisĕd'nagan'ob. (Nised, corruption of the French Lizett, or Elizabeth; Naganob, name of her father, who was chief at Fond du Lac, Minn.)

Mrs. Wa'wiĕkûm'ĭg[3]_____ Na'waji'bigo'kwe. (Central rock woman.)

Mrs. Star Bad Boy_____ Nenaka'wûbi'kwe. (Woman who is sitting with every other one.)

Wase'ya[4]_____ Light.

Mrs. Brunett[5]_____ Cai'yagose'. (Shaken loose.)

Mrs. Annie Davis_____ Ca'yabwûb'. (Sitting through.)

Mrs. Sharrett[6]_____ Ca'nodĕns. (Diminutive of Charlotte by slightly changing word and adding *ens*.)

Mrs. Sophia Agness_____ Memacka'wanamo'kwe. (Woman with a powerful respiration.)

Mrs. Margaret White.

Mrs. Roy.

Mrs. Mary Warren English.[7]

Mrs. Julia Warren Spears.[8]

Mrs. Sophia Warren.

Mrs. Charles Mee.

Albert Little Wolf[9]_____ Maiŋ'gans.

O'dĭni'gûn_____ Shoulder.

Ĕn'dûsogi'jĭg[10]_____ Every day.

Rev. Clement H. Beaulieu[11]____ Ḱa'waĕns (diminutive of his father's name Ka wa, which was the Chippewa mispronunciation of Clement).

PONSFORD, MINN. (WHITE EARTH RESERVATION)

Mrs. Fineday.

Mr. Rock[12]_____ A'sĭnĭ'okûm'ĭg. (Stony ground.)

Ne'yaji_____ Point of land.

Dĭ'kĕns_____ Diminutive of English "Dick."

Weza'waŋge_____ Yellow wing.

---

[1] The purpose of this list is to identify the persons who chiefly contributed to the material herewith presented. The name given first is therefore the name by which the person is generally known.

[2] Died October 23, 1919.

[3] Died September 16, 1923.

[4] Died April 4, 1921.

[5] Died April 29, 1926.

[6] Died April 14, 1925.

[7] Died August 15, 1925.

[8] Died June 21, 1925.

[9] Died April 6, 1927.

[10] Died October 24, 1926.

[11] Died July 4, 1926.

[12] Died January 21, 1920.

Mrs. Defoe_____ Meya'wigobiwĭk'. (Standing strongly.)
Mrs. Ward_____ Ni'gida'wananĭk'.
Mrs. Joker_____ Bewa'becodenisĭk'.
Mrs. Roy_____ Zo'zĕd (corruption of Josette).
Mrs. Roy (daughter of above)__ Ma'gidĭns (diminutive of Margaret).
Mrs. Lawrence.
Mrs. Gurneau.
Mrs. John English.
Mrs. Ca'wanokûm'igĭskûn'_____ Gi'wita'wisĕk'. (Walking around.)

Tom Skinaway_____ Manido'bijiki. (Spirit buffalo, or cattle.)
Mrs. Tom Skinaway_____ Na'cine'kwe.

William M. Rogers_____ Bĭn'dĭgegi'jĭg. (In the sky.)
Mrs. William M. Rogers_____ Bĭn'dige'ose'kwe. (Walking woman.)

Mrs. John Quaderer_____ Ogima'bĭnĕsi'kwe. (Chief bird woman.)

Mrs. Wilson.
Mrs. Lewis.

PHONETICS

ALPHABET

The vowels and consonants employed in this work do not represent every sound that occurs in the Chippewa language. Thus an obscure sound resembling *h* in the English alphabet sometimes occurs in the middle of a word and is not indicated. No attempt has been made to indicate a slight nasal sound that frequently occurs at the end of a word. Prolonged vowels are also not indicated. The following letters are used:

Vowels.—*a*, pronounced as in *father; e*, as in *they; ĕ* as in *met; i* as in *marine; ĭ*, as in *mint; o*, as in *note; u*, as in *rule; û*, as in *but; w*, as in *wan; y*, as in *yet.* If two consecutive vowels are pronounced separately, two dots are placed above the second vowel.

Diphthong.—*ai* pronounced as in *aisle.*

Consonants.—*b, d, f, k, m, n, p, s, t, v*, have the ordinary English sounds. *s* is always pronounced as in *sense, g* as in *get*, and *z* as in *zinc. c* represents the sound of *sh, j* the sound of *zh, tc* the sound of *tc* in *watch*, and *dj* the sound of *j* in *judge.*

a, PINE AND BALSAM TREES, WHITE EARTH, MINN.

b, TREES AT CASS LAKE

c, NORWAY PINES AT CASS LAKE

INTRODUCTION

A majority of the plants to be described in this paper were obtained on the White Earth Reservation in Minnesota. Specimens were also collected on the Red Lake, Cass Lake, Leech Lake, and Mille Lac Reservations in Minnesota, the Lac Court Oreilles Reservation in Wisconsin, and the Manitou Rapids Reserve in Ontario, Canada. Many of these were duplicates of plants obtained at White Earth but others were peculiar to the locality in which they were obtained.

The White Earth Reservation is located somewhat west of north-central Minnesota, on the border of the prairie that extends westward and forms part of the Great Plains. It also contains the lakes and pine forests that characterize northern Minnesota and extend into Canada. This produces an unusual variety of vegetation, so that the Chippewa living on other reservations are accustomed to go or send to White Earth for many of their medicinal herbs. Birch trees are found in abundance, either standing in groups (pl. 28), covering a hillside, or bordering a quiet lake. There are large tracts of sugar maples and forests of pine, cedar, balsam, and spruce. (Pl. 29.) Many of the lakes contain rice fields, and there are pretty, pebbly streams winding their way among overhanging trees. (Pl. 30.) Toward the west the prairie is dotted with little lakes or ponds, shining like mirrors. In June the air is sweet with wild roses and in midsummer the fields are beautiful with red lilies, bluebells, and a marvelous variety of color. In autumn the sumac flings its scarlet across the landscape and in winter there are miles of white, untrodden snow. The northern woodland is a beautiful country, and knowing it in all its changing seasons, one can not wonder at the poetry that is so inherent a part of Chippewa thought.

LIST OF PLANTS ARRANGED ACCORDING TO BOTANICAL NAME

Botanical name	Common name	Native name	Meaning	Use	Reference to use by other tribes [1]
Abies balsamea (L.) Mill.	balsam fir	a'ninandak'		medicine (headache)	
Acer saccharum Marsh.	sugar maple	a'nina'tig		food, utility	
Achillea millefolium L.	yarrow	a'djidamo'wano	squirrel tail	medicine (headache)	swelling, etc., Winnebago, 33d Rept. B. A. E., p. 134.
Acorus calamus L.	calamus	wikĕn' / na'bugŏck'	something flat	medicine (cold, etc.)	fever, cough, etc., 33d Rept. B. A. E., p. 69.
Actaea rubra (Ait.) Willd.	red baneberry	mŭckosīja'bosīgŭn	hay purgative	charm	
		wi'cosidji'blk	drawing root or plant	medicine (diseases of women).	
Agastache anethiodora (Nutt.) Britton.	giant hyssop	weza'wŭnŭckwŭk'	yellow plant	medicine (cough and pain in chest).	food, 33d Rept. B. A. E., p. 113.
Allionia nyctaginea Michx.	umbrella-plant	be'djukadak'igisīn	"it sticks up"	medicine (sprain)	fever, etc, 33d Rept. B. A. E., p. 78; fracture, Sioux, Bull. 61, p. 261.
Allium stellatum Ker	wild onion	mŭckode'cigaga'wŭnj	prairie skunk plant	medicine (colds)	
Allium tricoccum Ait.	wild leek	siga'gawŭnj'	onion	medicine (emetic)	
Alnus incana (L.) Moench	alder	wadŭb'		medicine (diseases of women), dye.	
Amelanchier canadensis (L.) Medic.	shadbush	guzigwa'kominaga'wŭnj	thorny wood	medicine (dysentery, diseases of women), food.	
Anaphalis margaritacea (L.) B. & H.	pearly everlasting	wa'bigwŭn	flowers	medicine (paralysis)	
Andropogon furcatus Muhl.	bluestem	mŭckode'kanĕs	small prairie	medicine (indigestion)	fever, etc, Omaha-Ponca, 33d Rept. B. A. E., p. 68.
Apocynum sp	dogbane	beba'mokodjibika'gisīn	"bear root, it is found here and there."	medicine (cough)	
Apocynum androsaemifolium L.	do	sass'bikwan / ma'kwona'gic odji'blk	bear entrails root.	medicine (heart palpitation, earache, headache; a baby's cold; also for charm).	
Aralia nudicaulis L.	wild sarsaparilla	wabos'odji'blk	rabbit root.	medicine (remedy for the blood, also applied to a sore), charm.	

Scientific name	Common name	Native name	Meaning	Use	Reference[1]
Aralia racemosa L.	spikenard	o'kadak'		medicine (cough), utility	
Arisaema triphyllum (L.) Torr.	Jack-in-the-pulpit	aya'bidjidji'bikŭgi'sin	(word implies adhesiveness)		
Arctium minus Bernh.	burdock	wi'sŭgtbŭg'	bitter leaf	medicine (sore eyes); medicine (cough), utility	pleurisy, 33d Rept. B. A. E., p. 135
Arctostaphylos uva-ursi (L.) Spreng.	bearberry	sagā'kominagŭnj'	berry with spikes	medicine (headache), food, utility, charm.	leaves smoked in pipe, 33d Rept. B. A. E., p.108.
Artemisia absinthium L.	wormwood	musē'odji'bĭk	worm root.	medicine (sprain)	
Artemisia dracunculoides Pursh.	mugwort	bŭ'giso'win; ba'sitnŭkrik'; jin'gwakwan'dŭg; i'ckodē'bŭg; ba'sibŭgŭk'; o'gima'wŭck.	swimming (bath); pine; fire leaf; small leaf; chief medicine.	medicine (dysentery, etc.)	fevers, etc., 33d Rept. B. A. E., p. 134.
Artemisia frigida Willd.	prairie sage	bi'jikiwŭn'gŭck	cattle herb.	medicine (convulsions, hemorrhage, tonic, and "antidote").	tonic, Chippewa, Bull. 53, p. 64; headache, Sioux, Bull. 61, p. 259; general medicinal, Missouri River tribes, 33d Rept. B. A. E., p. 134; indigestion, Tewa, Bull. 55, p. 54.
Artemisia gnaphalodes Nutt.	white mugwort	nokwe'iigŭn	something soft.		stomach trouble, 33d Rept. B. A. E., p. 134.
Asarum canadense L.	wild ginger	name'pin	sturgeon plant.	antidote, charm	
Asclepias incarnata L.	swamp milkweed	bi'giso'win	swimming.	medicine (indigestion), food, utility.	
Asclepias syriaca L.	common milkweed	inj'niwinj	"man-like".	medicine; medicine (diseases of women), food, charm.	food, 33d Rept. B. A. E., p. 139.
Aster (species doubtful)	aster	name'g osibŭg'	sturgeon leaf.	food	
Aster nemoralis Ait.	do	winj'sikèns	dirty, little.	medicine (disease of ear)	
Aster novae-angliae L.	do	do		charm	
Aster puniceus L.	do	do		do	
Astragalus crassicarpus Nutt.	ground-plum	bi'jikiwi'bŭgesan'	cattle plum.	medicine (convulsions and hemorrhages from wounds).	tonic, Chippewa, Bull. 53, p. 64.
Athyrium filix-foemina (L.) Roth.	lady fern	a'sawan		medicine (stoppage of urine)	
Betula nigra L.	black birch			medicine (pain in stomach)	

[1] Reference is made to the following works: Gilmore, Melvin Randolph, Uses of Plants by the Indians of the Missouri River Region, Thirty-third Ann. Rept. Bur. Amer. Ethn.; Robbins, Harrington, and Friere-Marreco, Ethnobotany of the Tewa Indians, Bull. 55, Bur. Amer. Ethn.; Swanton, John R., Religious Beliefs and Medical Practices of the Creek Indians, Forty-second Ann. Rept. Bur. Amer. Ethn., pp. 655-670; and Bulls. 53 and 61, Bur. Amer. Ethn., by the present writer.

LIST OF PLANTS ARRANGED ACCORDING TO BOTANICAL NAME—Continued

Botanical name	Common name	Native name	Meaning	Use	Reference to use by other tribes
Betula papyrifera Marsh	white birch	wi'gwass'tíg		medicine (pain in stomach), utility.	utility, Sioux, 33d Rept. B. A. E., p. 75.
Botrychium virginianum (L.) Sw.	rattlesnake fern			medicine (bites)	
Bovista pila B. C. C				charm	
Bursa bursa-pastoris (L.) Britton	shepherd's-purse	i'ckode'wadji'bik	fire root	medicine (dysentery)	
Caltha palustris L	cowslip	o'gite'big		medicine (scrofulous sores)	
Calvatia craniiformis Schw	puffball			medicine (nosebleed)	
Campanula rotundifolia L	harebell (Scotch blue-bell).	zi'gini'ce	(zigin implies pouring)	medicine (disease of ear)	
Castalia odorata (Ait.) Woodv. & Wood.	white waterlily		root	medicine (sore mouth)	
Castilleja coccinea (L.) Spreng	painted-cup	Winabojo' noko'mis wi'-nizisin'	Winabojo's grandmother's hair.	medicine (rheumatism and diseases of women).	
Caulophyllum thalictroides (L.) Michx.	blue cohosh	be'cigodji'bigúk	one root	medicine (lung trouble and cramps).	fever, Omaha, 33d Rept. B. A. E., p. 83.
Ceanothus ovatus Desf	New Jersey tea	odiga'dimanido'		medicine (lung trouble and emetic).	
Celastrus scandens L	bittersweet	bima'kwûd	twisting around	medicine (physic and eruptions).	poisonous, Sioux, 33d Rept. B. A. E., p. 102.
Chimaphila umbellata (L.) Nutt.	pipsissewa	ga'gige'búg	everlasting leaf	medicine (disease of eye)	
Chiogenes hispidula (L.) T. & G	creeping snowberry	wabos'obigons'	small rabbit-leaf	food	
Cicuta maculata L	poison hemlock	wanikons'		smoked	
Cirsium species	thistle	ma'zana'tíg		medicine (diseases of women)	
Clintonia borealis (Ait.) Raf	clintonia			medicine (sore and burn), amusement.	
Coptis trifolia (L.) Salisb	goldthread	oza'widji'bik	yellow root	dye	
Cornus alternifolia L. f	dogwood	muj'omij'	moose plant	medicine (disease of eye), utility, charm.	
Cornus canadensis L	bunchberry	caca'gomin		food	
Cornus rugosa Lam	dogwood			smoked	
Cornus stolonifera Michx	red-osier dogwood	mis'kwabi'mic	reddish	medicine (eyes), utility, dye.	smoked in pipe, 33d Rept. B. A. E., p. 108.

Corylus americana Walt.	hazel	bagan'	nut, bark, burs, and wood	food, dye, and utility	food, 33d Rept. B. A. E., p. 74.
Corylus rostrata Ait.	...do...	...do...	...do...	utility and medicine (lungs)	
Crataegus species	thornapple	mine'sagawŭnj	having fruit and also spikes	food, utility, medicine (diseases of women).	
Cucurbita maxima Duchesne	squash	na'bâgogwis'simain	flat pumpkin	food	
Cucurbita pepo L.	pumpkin	ogwis'simain		...do...	
Cypripedium hirsutum Mill.	ladyslipper	ago'biso'win	word refers to sewing	medicine (toothache)	
Dicranum bonjeanii De Not.	woodmoss			utility	
Diervilla lonicera Mill.	bush honeysuckle			medicine (stomach trouble)	
Dirca palustris L.	moosewood	djibe'gŭb	first two syllables mean ghost or spirit.	medicine (physic)	
Drymocallis arguta (Pursh) Rydb	five-finger	gi'tcîôde'iminidji'bîk	big heart-berry root	medicine (headache)	
Epilobium angustifolium L.	fireweed	oja'cidji'bîk	slippery root	medicine (bruise)	
Equisetum hiemale L.	scouring-rush	gijib'inûskon'	"It is round"	utility	
Equisetum praealtum Raf.	...do...	...do...	...do...	...do...	
Erigeron canadensis L.	horseweed	gababi'kwûns'tîg	knotted tree.	medicine (pain in stomach, diseases of women).	
Erysimum cheiranthoides L.	wormseed mustard	o'zawa'bigwûn	yellow flower	medicine (eruptions)	
Eupatorium maculatum L.	Joe-Pye-weed	me'skwana'kûk bû'giso'win.	swimming	medicine (strengthening baths)	
Eupatorium perfoliatum L.	boneset	niya'wîbûkûk'		charm	
Euthamia graminifolia (L.) Nutt.	goldenrod			medicine (pain in chest)	
Falcata comosa (L.) Kuntze	hog peanut	bûgwûdj'mîskodî'simîn	unusual, reddish bean	medicine (physic)	food, 33d Rept. B. A. E., p. 95.
Fomes applanatus	shell fungus			toys	
Fragaria virginiana Duchesne	wild strawberry	ode'iminidji'bîk	heart berry root	medicine (cholera-infantum)	food, 33d Rept. B. A. E., p. 84.
Fraxinus species	ash	a'gimak'	snowshoe wood	medicine (tonic), utility	
Fraxinus nigra Marsh	black ash			utility	
Gaultheria procumbens L.	wintergreen	winî'sîbûgons'	dirty leaf	food	
Geranium maculatum L.	wild geranium	be'cigodji'bigrûk	one root	medicine (sore mouth), food	
Geum canadense Jacq	avens			medicine (diseases of women)	
Grossularia oxyacanthoides (L.) Mill.	gooseberry	cabo'minaga'wûnj	smooth berry	...do...	
Helianthus tuberosus L.	Jerusalem artichoke	a'skibwan'	raw thing	food	food, 33d Rept. B. A. E., p. 131.
Heliopsis scabra Dunal	ox-eye	gi'gîso'bûgons'	sun, small leaf	medicine (tonic)	
Hepatica americana Ker.	hepatica	gabîsan'îkeag'	"it is silent"	medicine (convulsions)	
Hepatica triloba L.	...do...	animr'sîd		charm	
Heracleum lanatum Michx.	cow parsnip	bi'bigwe'wînûck	flute-reed	medicine (indigestion, boils, and sore throat).	boils, 33d Rept. B. A. E., p. 107.
Heuchera (species doubtful)	alum-root	ciwade'imîn'îbûg	sour leaf	medicine (sore mouth)	

LIST OF PLANTS ARRANGED ACCORDING TO BOTANICAL NAME—Continued

Botanical name	Common name	Native name	Meaning	Use	Reference to use by other tribes
Heuchera hispida Pursh	alum-root	ciwade'iminaga'wûnj	sour fruit	medicine (indigestion and diseases of eye)	dysentery, Sioux, Bull. 61, p. 269.
Hicoria alba (L.) Britton	hickory	mî'tigwabak'	bow-wood	utility and medicine (headache).	
Hordeum jubatum L.	squirrel-tail	a'djidamo'wano	squirrel-tail	medicine (sty on eye)	
Iris versicolor L.	blueflag			medicine (poultice)	
Juglans cinerea L.	butternut			dye	
Juniperus communis L.	juniper	ga'gawan'dagisîd	deceptive	utility	
Juniperus virginiana L.*	red cedar	miskwa'wak	red wood	medicine, utility	
Koellia virginiana (L.) MacM.	mountain mint	name'wûckons'	little sturgeon plant	medicine (fevers and diseases of women), food.	
Lacinaria scariosa (L.) Kuntze	blazing-star	o'mucko'zowa'no	elk tail	medicine (diseases of the horse).	dysentery, 33d Rept. B. A. E, p. 133.
Lactuca canadensis L.	wild lettuce	odjici'gomin		medicine (warts)	
Larix laricina (Du Roi) Koch	tamarack	mû'ckigwa'tig	swamp tree	medicine (burns), utility.	
Lathyrus venosus Muhl	wild pea	mî'nîsîno'wûck	island medicine	medicine (convulsions and hemorrhage from wounds), food, charm.	
Ledum groenlandicum Oeder	Labrador tea	muckig'obûg	swamp leaf	medicine (ulcers), food	
Leptandra virginica (L.) Nutt.	culver's-root	wî'sûgidji'bîk	bitter root	medicine (physic)	
Lilium canadense L.	lily	Winabojo'bikwûk'	Winabojo's arrow	medicine (snake bite)	
Lithospermum carolinense (Walt.) MacM.	puccoon	odji'bîknamîn'		dye	
Lonicera sp	honeysuckle			medicine (lung trouble)	
Lycopodium obscurum L.	ground-pine			medicine (stiff joints)	
Lycopus asper Greene	bugleweed	ande'gopîn	crow plant	food	
Monarda mollis L.	horsemint	bibî'gwûnûkûk' wabino'wûck	resembling a flute, eastern medicine	medicine (eruptions, burns, and worms).	
Nepeta cataria L.	catnip	gajugêns'îbûg	little-cat leaf	medicine (fevers).	
Onosmodium hispidissimum Mackenzie	false gromwell	mî'gîsêns'îbûg	little-shell leaf	charm	
Osmorrhiza claytoni Michx.	sweet cicely	osaga'tigom'	tangled branches	medicine (ulcers and sore throat).	

Scientific name	Common name	Chippewa name	Meaning	Use	Reference
Ostrya virginiana (Mill.) Koch	hop hornbeam, ironwood.	ma'nanons'		medicine (kidney trouble)	
Oxycoccus macrocarpus (Ait.) Pers.*	cranberry	a'nibimīn'		food	
Parthenocissus quinquefolia (L.) Greene.	woodbine	manido'bima'kwūd.		do	food, 33d Rept. B. A. E., p. 102.
Petalostemon purpureus (Vent.) Rydb.	prairie-clover	ba'sibûgûk'	small leaves	medicine (heart trouble)	
Phragmites communis Trin.	reed	abo'djigûn	"something turned out or over."	utility	utility, Tewa, Bull. 55, p. 66.
Phryma leptostachya L.	lopseed			medicine (sore throat)	
Picea canadensis (Mill.) B. S. P.	white spruce			medicine (stiff joints)	
Picea rubra (DuRoi) Dietr	spruce	cingob'		utility	
Pinus resinosa Ait.	red pine	jïngwak'		do	
Pinus strobus L.	white pine	...do...		do	
Plantago major L.	plantain	gine'biwûck / o'mûkîk'ībûg	snake-like / frog leaf	medicine (inflammation) / charm	used as an application to draw out splinter, Omaha-Ponca, 33d Rept. B. A. E., p. 115.
Polygala senega L.	Seneca snakeroot	bi'jikiwûck'	cattle medicine	medicine (tonic), charm	tonic, Chippewa, Bull. 53, p. 64.
Polygonatum commutatum (R. & S.) Dietr.	Solomonseal			medicine (headache)	
Polygonum persicaria L.	smartweed	ojig'imin		medicine (pain in stomach)	
Polygonum punctatum Ell	do	man'asa'dî	fisher-berry	do	
Populus balsamifera L.	balsam poplar	asa'dî		medicine (heart trouble), charm.	
Populus tremuloides Michx.	aspen	bine'bûg.	prairie chicken or grouse leaf.	medicine (diseases of women) food.	urinary system, Tewa, Bull. 55, p. 42.
Potentilla palustris (L.) Scop.	marshlocks			medicine (dysentery)	
Potentilla monspeliensis L.	cinquefoil	dado'cabodjî'bîk	"milk-root"	medicine (sore throat)	
Prenanthes alba L.	rattlesnake-root	namē'wiskons'		medicine (diseases of women)	
Prunella vulgaris L.	selfheal			do	
Prunus (species doubtful)				do	
Prunus americana Marsh	wild plum	bû'gesana'tîg.		medicine (disinfectant), food.	food, medicine, and utility, 33d Rept. B. A. E., p. 87.
Prunus serotina Ehrh.	wild cherry	ikwe'mîc.		medicine (digestive troubles, etc.), food.	
Prunus virginiana L.	chokecherry	a'sisûwe'mïnaga'wûnj.		do	

* Plants are marked with an asterisk if specimens were not submitted.

LIST OF PLANTS ARRANGED ACCORDING TO BOTANICAL NAME—Continued

Botanical name	Common name	Native name	Meaning	Use	Reference to use by other tribes
Psoralea argophylla Pursh	psoralea	gi'ziso'bûgons'	sun, little leaf	medicine (diseases of the horse)	
Pulsatilla hirsutissima (Pursh) Britton.	pasque-flower	gogeda'djibûg		medicine (headache, etc.)	
Quercus species	oak	mitigo'mizinc		utility	food, 33d Rept. B. A. E., p. 75.
Quercus macrocarpa Muhl	bur oak	mi'tigo'mic		medicine (wounds), food	food, Tewa, Bull. 55, p. 107 (footnote).
Quercus rubra L	red oak	wi'sugi'mitigo'mic	bitter oak	medicine (heart), food	
Rhus glabra L	sumac	maki'bûg		medicine (dysentery)	dysentery, etc., also dye, 33d Rept. B. A. E., p. 99.
Rhus hirta (L.) Sudw	staghorn sumac			utility, dye, medicine (pain in stomach).	
Ribes glandulosum Gauer	wild currant	wabos'odji'bîk	rabbit leaf	medicine (diseases of women)	
Ribes triste Pall	red currant	cigagwa'tigon	skunk-like	medicine (gravel), food	
Ribes species	wild currant	micidji'minaga'wûnj	fuzzy fruit	medicine (urinary trouble), food.	
Rosa arkansana Porter	wild rose	bi'jikiwi'ginîg	cattle rose	medicine (tonic, etc.)	
Rosa species	rose	ogini'minaga'wûnj	rose berries	medicine (diseases of eye), food.	
Rubus occidentalis L	black raspberry	oda'tagago'minaga'wûnj		medicine (diseases of women)	
Rubus frondosus Bigel. (?)	blackberry	do		medicine (lung trouble), food.	
Rubus strigosus Michx	red raspberry	mis'kominaga'wûnj	having reddish berries	medicine (diseases of eye, diseases of women; also dysentery).	
Rudbeckia laciniata L	cone-flower	gi'ziswe'bîgwa'ls	"it is scattering"	medicine (indigestion and burns).	
		gi'ziso'bûgons'	sun, little leaf		
Rumex obtusifolius L	bitter dock	oza'widji'bîk	yellow root	medicine (cuts, ulcers)	
Rumex crispus L	yellow dock	ginoje'wûkûn	pike plant	medicine (eruptions)	
		oza'widji'bîk	yellow root		
Sagittaria latifolia Willd	arrowhead	muj'ota'bûk	moose leaf	medicine (indigestion), food	
Salix species	willow	ozi'sigo'bimîc		medicine (indigestion), utility	utility, 33d Rept. B. A. E., p. 73.

Sanguinaria canadensis L.	bloodroot	mîs'kodjî'bîk	red root	dye, medicine	dye and charm, 33d Rept. B. A. E., p. 83.
Sanicula canadensis L.	bur snakeroot	mîkî'ûde'wîdjî'bîk	black root	medicine (diseases of women)	
Sarracenia purpurea L.	pitcher-plant	o'mîkîkî'wîda'stîn	frog leggings	amusement	
Scirpus validus Vahl	bulrush	ana'kûn		utility, food	food, 33d Rept. B. A. E., p. 69.
Sieversia ciliata (Pursh) Rydb	prairie-smoke	ne'baneya'nekweâg	"it is one-sided"	medicine (tonic and stimulant).	
Silphium perfoliatum L.	cup-plant	akûn'damo	watcher, or spy	medicine (hemorrhages)	rheumatism, 33d Rept. B. A. E., p. 132.
Smilax herbacea L.	carrion-flower	ma'kodjî'bîk	bear root	medicine (physic and urinary system).	food and remedy for hoarseness, 33d. Rept. B. A. E., p. 71.
Solidago species	goldenrod	gî'zîso'mûkî'kî	sun medicine	medicine (fever, ulcers and boils).	calendar flower, 33d Rept. B. A. E., p. 133.
Solidago altissima L.	do	a'djîdamo'wano	squirrel tail	medicine (cramps)	ceremonial, Tewa, Bull. 55, p. 49 (footnote).
Solidago flexicaulis L.	do	do	do	medicine (diseases of women)	
Solidago juncea Ait	do	do	do	medicine (convulsions and diseases of women).	
Solidago rigida L.	do	do	do	medicine (urinary trouble)	
Solidago rigidiuscula Porter	do	o'zawa'bîgwîn	yellow flower	medicine (lung trouble)	
Sphagnum species	sphagnum	asa'kûmîg		utility	
Stachys palustris L.	hedge-nettle	ande'gobîg	crow leaf	medicine (colic)	
Stellaria media (L.) Cyrill	chickweed	wî'nîbîdja'bîbaga'no	toothplant	medicine (sore eyes)	
Streptopus roseus Michx	twisted-stalk	agwîn'gûsîbûg	ground-squirrel leaf	medicine (sty on eye)	
Symphoricarpos albus (L.) Blake.	snowberry	maîŋ'gamîna'tîg	wolf wood	medicine (physic)	
Tanacetum vulgare L.	tansy	o'ckîngî'kweânî'bîc	young woman's leaf	medicine (sore throat, diseases of women, fevers, and for soreness of ear).	
Taraxacum officinale Weber	dandelion	dado'cabodjî'bîk	milk root	medicine (diseases of women)	
Taxus canadensis Marsh	yew	ne'bagandag'	"it is one-sided"	medicine (rheumatism)	
Thaspium barbinode (Michx.) Nutt.	meadow parsnip	bûsîdjî'bîktîgnîk	plump root	medicine (colic)	
Thuja occidentalis L.	arborvitae (white cedar).	gî'jîkan'dûg	cedar-like	medicine (cough)	
Tilia americana L.	basswood	wîgub'îmîj		utility	utility, 33d Rept. B. A. E., p. 102.

LIST OF PLANTS ARRANGED ACCORDING TO BOTANICAL NAME—Continued

Botanical name	Common name	Native name	Meaning	Use	Reference to use by other tribes
Torresia odorata (L.) Hitche.	sweetgrass	wicko'bimŭcko'si	sweet grass	ceremonial, pleasure, utility	
Trillium grandiflorum (Michx.) Salisb.	wake-robin	in'nīwīn'dībīge'gŭn		medicine (rheumatism, cramps, and soreness of ear)	
Tsuga canadensis (L.) Carr.	hemlock	gaga'gimīc		medicine (hemorrhage from wounds), food, dye	
Typha latifolia L.	cat-tail	apŭk'we		utility	utility, 33d Rept. B. A. E., p. 64; Tewa, Bull. 55, p. 66.
Ulmus fulva Michx.	slippery elm	gawa'komīc		medicine (sore throat), utility	laxative, food, and utility, 33d Rept. B. A. E., p. 76.
Urtica gracilis Ait.	nettle	ma'zana'tĭg, bepadji'-ckanakiz'ĭt ma'zana'tĭg.	a prickly nettle	medicine (urinary system and dysentery).	utility, 33d Rept. B. A. E., p. 77.
Urticastrum divaricatum (L.) Kuntze.	false nettle	ze'sŭb		utility	
Vaccinium angustifolium Alt.	blueberry	mĭn'aga'wĭnj		medicine ("craziness"), food	
Vagnera racemosa (L.) Morong.	false Solomonseal	agoŋg'osiminĭn'		medicine (diseases of women)	
Verbena hastata L.	vervain			medicine (nosebleed)	
Veronica virginica L.		wi'sŭgĭdjī'bĭk	bitter root	medicine (nosebleed, scrofula)	
Viburnum acerifolium L.	arrowwood	anib'		medicine (emetic)	
Viburnum pauciflorum Pylaie.	highland cranberry			food	
Vitis cordifolia Michx.	grape	jo'minaga'wŭnj		medicine, food	
Zanthoxylum americanum Mill.	prickly ash	gawa'komīc		medicine (sore throat)	
Zea mays L.	corn	manda'mĭn		food	
Zizania palustris L.¹	wild rice	mano'mĭn		do	

¹ Zizania aquatica, a variety of wild rice having smaller heads and slightly smaller grains than Zizania palustris is also found in northern Minnesota.

LIST OF PLANTS ARRANGED ACCORDING TO COMMON NAME

Common name [1]	Botanical name	Common name	Botanical name
Alder	Alnus incana (L.) Moench.	Cranberry, highland	Viburnum pauciflorum Pylaie.
Alum-root	Heuchera (species doubtful).	Culver's-root	Leptandra virginica (L.) Nutt.
Alum-root	Heuchera hispida Pursh.		
Arborvitae (white cedar).	Thuja occidentalis L.	Cup-plant	Silphium perfoliatum L.
Artichoke, Jerusalem	Helianthus tuberosus L.	Currant, red	Ribes triste Pall.
Arrowhead	Sagittaria latifolia Willd.	Currant, wild	Ribes species.
Arrowwood	Viburnum acerifolium L.	Currant, wild	Ribes glandulosum Gauer.
Ash	Fraxinus species.	Dandelion	Taraxacum officinale Weber.
Ash, black	Fraxinus nigra Marsh.	Dock, bitter	Rumex obtusifolius L.
Ash, prickly	Zanthoxylum americanum Mill.	Dock, yellow	Rumex crispus L.
		Dogbane	Apocynum species.
Aspen	Populus tremuloides Michx.	Dogbane	Apocynum androsaemifolium L.
Aster	Aster (species doubtful).		
Aster	Aster nemoralis Ait.	Dogwood	Cornus alternifolia L. f.
Aster	Aster novae-angliae L.	Dogwood	Cornus rugosa Lam.
Aster	Aster puniceus L	Dogwood, red-osier	Cornus stolonifera Michx.
Avens	Geum canadense Jacq.	Elm, slippery	Ulmus fulva Michx.
Baneberry, red	Actaea rubra (Ait.) Willd.	False Solomonseal	Vagnera racemosa (L.) Morong.
Basswood	Tilia americana L.		
Bearberry	Arctostaphylos uva-ursi (L.) Spreng.	Fern, lady	Athyrium filix-foemina (L.) Roth.
Birch, black	Betula nigra L.	Fern, rattlesnake	Botrychium virginianum (L.) Sw.
Birch, white	Betula papyrifera Marsh.		
Bittersweet	Celastrus scandens L.	Fir, balsam	Abies balsamea (L.) Mill.
Blackberry	Rubus frondosus Bigel. (?)	Fireweed	Epilobium angustifolium L.
Blazing-star	Lacinaria scariosa (L.) Kuntze.	Five-finger	Drymocallis arguta (Pursh) Rydb.
Bloodroot	Sanguinaria canadensis L.	Fungus, shelf	Fomes applanatus.
Bluebell, (Scotch harebell).	Campanula rotundifolia L.	Geranium, wild	Geranium maculatum L.
		Ginger, wild	Asarum canadense L.
Blueberry	Vaccinium angustifolium Ait.	Goldenrod	Euthamia graminifolia (L.) Nutt.
Blueflag	Iris versicolor L.		
Bluestem	Andropogon furcatus Muhl.	Goldenrod	Solidago altissima L.
Boneset	Eupatorium perfoliatum L.	Goldenrod	Solidago flexicaulis L.
Bugle-weed	Lycopus asper Greene.	Goldenrod	Solidago juncea Ait.
Bulrush	Scirpus validus Vahl.	Goldenrod	Solidago rigida L.
Bunchberry	Cornus canadensis L.	Goldenrod	Solidago rigidiuscula Porter.
Burdock	Arctium minus Bernh.	Goldenrod	Solidago species.
Butternut	Juglans cinerea L.	Goldthread	Coptis trifolia (L.) Salisb.
Calamus	Acorus calamus L.	Gooseberry	Grossularia oxyacanthoides (L.) Mill.
Carrion-flower	Smilax herbacea L.		
Catnip	Nepeta cataria L.	Grape	Vitis cordifolia Michx.
Cat-tail	Typha latifolia L.	Gromwell, false	Onosmodium hispidissimum Mackenzie.
Cedar, red	Juniperus virginiana L.*		
Cedar, white (arborvitae).	Thuja occidentalis L.	Ground-pine	Lycopodium obscurum L.
		Ground-plum	Astragalus crassicarpus Nutt.
Cherry, wild	Prunus serotina Ehrh.		
Chickweed	Stellaria media (L.) Cyrill.	Harebell (Scotch bluebell).	Campanula rotundifolia L.
Chokecherry	Prunus virginiana L.		
Cicely, sweet	Osmorrhiza claytoni Michx.	Hazel	Corylus americana Walt.
Cinquefoil	Potentilla monspeliensis L.	Hazel	Corylus rostrata Ait.
Clintonia	Clintonia borealis Ait. (Canadian specimen).	Hedge-nettle	Stachys palustris L.
		Hemlock	Tsuga canadensis (L.) Carr.
Cohosh, blue	Caulophyllium thalictroides (L.) Michx.	Hemlock, poison	Cicuta maculata L.
		Hepatica	Hepatica americana Ker.
Cone-flower	Rudbeckia laciniata L.	Hepatica	Hepatica triloba L.
Corn	Zea mays L.	Hickory	Hicoria alba (L.) Britton.
Cowslip	Caltha palustris L.	Honeysuckle	Lonicera species.
Cranberry	Oxycoccus macrocarpus (Ait.) Pers.*	Honeysuckle, bush	Diervilla lonicera Mill.

[1] Attention is directed to the fact that the common name of a plant frequently differs in different localities and that, in some instances, a plant is known by more than one common name. The list herewith presented contains the names by which the plants are most widely known.

* Plants are marked with an asterisk if specimens were not submitted.

LIST OF PLANTS ARRANGED ACCORDING TO COMMON NAME—Continued

Common name	Botanical name	Common name	Botanical name
Hornbeam, hop (ironwood).	Ostrya virginiana (Mill.) Koch.	Puccoon	Lithospermum carolinense (Walt.) MacM.
Horsemint	Monarda mollis L.	Puffball	Calvatia craniiformis Schw.
Horseweed	Erigeron canadensis L.	Pumpkin	Cucurbita pepo L.
Hyssop, giant	Agastache anethiodora (Nutt.) Britton.	Raspberry, black	Rubus occidentalis L.
		Raspberry, red	Rubus strigosus Michx.
Ironwood (hop hornbeam).	Ostrya virginiana (Mill.) Koch.	Rattlesnake-root	Prenanthes alba L.
		Reed	Phragmites communis Trin.
Jack-in-the-pulpit	Arisaema triphyllum (L.) Torr.	Rice, wild	Zizania palustris L.
		Rose	Rosa species.
Joe Pye weed	Eupatorium maculatum L.	Rose, wild	Rosa arkansana Porter.
June berry (shadbush).	Amelanchier canadensis (L.) Medic.	Sage, prairie	Artemisia frigida Willd.
		Sarsaparilla, wild	Aralia nudicaulis L.
Juniper	Juniperus communis L.	Scouring-rush	Equisetum hiemale L.
Ladyslipper	Cypripedium hirsutum Mill.	Scouring-rush	Equisetum praecaltum Raf.
Leek, wild	Allium tricoccum Ait.	Selfheal	Prunella vulgaris L.
Lettuce, wild	Lactuca canadensis L.	Shadbush	Amelanchier canadensis (L.) Medic.
Lily	Lilium canadense L.		
Lily, white water	Castalia odorata (Ait.) Woodv. & Wood.	Shepherd's-purse	Bursa bursa-pastoris (L.) Britton.
Lopseed	Phryma leptostachya L.	Smartweed	Polygonum persicaria L.
Maple, sugar	Acer saccharum Marsh.	Smartweed	Polygonum punctatum Ell.
Marshlocks	Potentilla palustris (L.) Scop.	Snakeroot, bur	Sanicula canadensis L.
Milkweed, common	Asclepias syriaca L.	Snakeroot, Seneca	Polygala senega L.
Milkweed, swamp	Asclepias incarnata L.	Snowberry	Symphoricarpos albus (L.) Blake.
Mint, mountain	Koellia virginiana (L.) MacM		
Moosewood	Dirca palustris L.	Snowberry, creeping.	Chiogenes hispidula (L.) T. & G.
Mugwort	Artemisia dracunculoides Pursh.	Solomonseal	Polygonatum commutatum.
		Sphagnum	Sphagnum species.
Mugwort	Artemisia gnaphalodes Nutt.	Spikenard	Aralia racemosa L.
Mustard, wormseed	Erysimum cheiranthoides L.	Spruce	Picea rubra (Du Roi) Dietr.
Nettle	Urtica gracilis Ait.	Spruce, white	Picea canadensis (Mill.) B. S. P.
Nettle, false	Urticastrum divaricatum (L.) Kuntze.	Squash	Cucurbita maxima Duchesne.
Oak	Quercus species.		
Oak, bur	Quercus macrocarpa Muhl.	Squirrel-tail	Hordeum jubatum L.
Oak, red	Quercus rubra L.	Strawberry, wild	Fragaria virginiana Duchesne.
Onion, wild	Allium stellatum Ker.		
Ox-eye	Heliopsis scabra Dunal.	Sumac	Rhus glabra L.
Painted-cup	Castilleja coccinea (L.) Spreng.	Sumac, staghorn	Rhus hirta (L.) Sudw.
		Sweetgrass	Torresia odorata(L.) Hitche.
Parsnip, cow	Heracleum lanatum Michx.	Tamarack	Larix laricina (Du Roi) Koch.
Parsnip, meadow	Thaspium barbinode (Michx.) Nutt.	Tansy	Tanacetum vulgare L.
		Tea, Labrador	Ledum groenlandicum Oeder.
Pasque-flower	Pulsatilla hirsutissima (Pursh.) Britton.		
		Tea, New Jersey	Ceanothus ovatus Desf.
Pea, wild	Lathyrus venosus Muhl.	Thistle	Cirsium species.
Peanut, hog	Falcata comosa (L.) Kuntze.	Thornapple	Crataegus species.
Pearly everlasting	Anaphalis margaritacea (L.) B. & H.	Twisted-stalk	Streptopus roseus Michx.
		Umbrella-plant	Allionia nyctaginea Michx.
Pine, red	Pinus resinosa Ait.	Vervain	Verbena hastata L.
Pine, white	Pinus strobus L.	Wake-robin	Trillium grandiflorum (Michx.) Salisb.
Pipsissewa	Chimaphila umbellata (L.) Nutt.		
Pitcher-plant	Sarracenia purpurea L.	Willow	Salix species.
Plantain	Plantago major L.	Willow, spotted	Salix species.
Plum, wild	Prunus americana Marsh.	Wintergreen	Gaultheria procumbens L.
Poplar, balsam	Populus balsamifera L.	Woodbine	Parthenocissus quinquefolia (L.) Greene.
Prairie-clover	Petalostemon purpureus (Vent.) Rydb.		
		Woodmoss	Dicranum bonjeanii De Not.
Prairie smoke	Sieversia ciliata (Pursh) Rydb.	Wormwood	Artemisia absinthium L.
		Yarrow	Achillea millefolium L.
Psoralea	Psoralea argophylla Pursh.	Yew	Taxus canadensis Marsh.

There is no exact terminology of Chippewa plants, although there are some generally accepted designations of common plants and trees. In obtaining the names of plants it was found that the same name is often given to several plants, and that one plant may have several names. Individuals often had their own names for the plants which they used as remedies. It was also customary for a medicine man, when teaching the use of a plant, to show a specimen of the plant without giving it any name. Thus the identity of the plant was transmitted with more secrecy than would have been possible if a name had been assigned to it. The names by which plants are designated by the Chippewa are usually compound nouns indicating the appearance of the plant, the place where it grows, a characteristic property of the plant, or its principal use. To this is often added a termination indicating the part of the plant which is utilized, as root or leaf.

Examples of these classes of plant names are as follows:

Name indicating appearance of the plant: Be'cigodji'bigŭk (blue cohosh), *becig*, one; *djibiguk*, root; the plant having a tap root.

Name indicating place where the plant grows: Mŭ'ckigwa'tĭg (tamarack), *muckig*, swamp; *atig*, termination indicating wood.

Name indicating a characteristic property of the plant: Dado'cabodji'bĭk (dandelion), *dadocabo*, liquid, or milk; *odjibik*, root.

Name indicating characteristic use of plant: A'gimak' (ash), *agim*, snowshoe; *ak*, termination signifying wood.

LIST OF PLANTS [1] ARRANGED ACCORDING TO NATIVE NAME

Native name	Common name	Native name	Common name
Abo'djigŭn	Reed.	A'sĭsûwe'mĭnaga'wûnj	Chokecherry.
A'djidamo'wano	Yarrow, squirrel - tail, goldenrod.[1]	Aya'bĭdjidji'bikûgi'sĭn	Spikenard.
		Bagan'	
A'gimak'	Ash.	Ba'sibûgŭk'	Mugwort, prairie clover.
Ago'bisowĭn	Ladyslipper.	Ba'sûnûkûk'	Mugwort.
Agoŋg'osimĭnûn'	False Solomonseal.	Beba'mokodjibika'gisĭn	Dogbane.
Agwĭn'gûsibûg'	Twisted-stalk.	Be'cigodji'bigŭk	Blue cohosh, wild geranium.
Akûn'damo	Cup-plant.		
Aṇa'kûn	Bulrush.	Be'dukadak'igisĭn	Umbrella plant.
Ande'gobûg	Hedge-nettle.	Bepadji'ckanakĭz'ĭt ma'-zana'tĭg.	Nettle.
Ande'gopĭn	Honeysuckle, bugleweed.	Bi'bigwe'wûnûck	Cow parsnip.
Anib'	Arrowwood.	Bibi'gwûnûkûk'	Horsemint.
Anib'icĕns'	Goldenrod.	Bi'jikiwi'bûgesan'	Ground-plum.
A'nibimĭn'	Cranberry.	Bi'jikiwi'ginĭg	Wild rose.
Anib'imĭnûga'wûnj		Bi'jikiwĭn'gûck	Prairie sage.
Anidji'mĭnĭbûg'		Bi'jikiwûck'	Seneca snakeroot.
A'ninandak'	Balsam fir.	Bima'kwûd	Bittersweet.
A'nina'tĭg	Sugar maple.	Bĭne'bûg	Marsh locks.
A'nimu'sĭd	Hepatica.	Bû'gesana'tĭg	Wild plum.
Apûk'we	Cat-tail.	Bû'giso'wĭn	Mugwort, swamp milkweed, Joe Pye weed.
Asa'dĭ	Aspen.		
Asa'kûmĭg	Wood-moss, sphagnum.	Bûgwûdj'mĭskodi'sĭmĭn	Hog peanut.
A'sawan	Lady fern.	Bûsidji'bĭkûgûk	Meadow parsnip.
As'kibwan'	Jerusalem artichoke.	Cabo'mĭnaga'wûnj	Gooseberry.

[1] It will be noted that one name is frequently given to several plants and that one plant is frequently called by several names.

LIST OF PLANTS ARRANGED ACCORDING TO NATIVE NAME—Continued

Native name	Common name	Native name	Common name
Caca'gomĭn	Bunch berry.	Mŭckode'cigaga'wûnj	Wild onion.
Cigagwa'tĭgon	Red currant.	Mŭckode'kanĕs	Bluestem.
Cĭngob'	Spruce.	Mŭ'ckosija'bosigûn	Calamus.
Ciwade'imĭn'Ĭbûg	Alum-root.	Mûj'omĭj	Dogwood.
Ciwade'imĭnaga'wûnj	Alum-root.	Mûj'ota'bûk	Arrowhead.
Dado'cabodji'bĭk	Rattlesnake-root, dandelion.	Mŭkûde'widji'bĭk	Bur snake root.
		Muse'odji'bĭk	Wormwood.
Djibe'gûb	Moosewood.	Ne'bagandag'	Yew.
Gababi'kwûna'tĭg	Horseweed.	Na'bûgogwis'simaûn'	Squash.
Gabisan'ikeäg'	Hepatica.	Na'bugûck'	Calamus.
Gaga'gimĭc	Hemlock.	Name'gosibûg'	Aster.
Ga'gawan'dagisĭd	Juniper.	Name'pĭn	Wild ginger.
Ga'gige'bûg	Pipsissewa.	Name'wûckons	Mountain mint (also selfheal).
Ga'jugĕns'Ĭbûg	Catnip.		
Gawa'komĭc	Slippery elm, prickly ash.	Ne'baneya'nekweäg'	Prairie smoke.
Gijib'inûskon'	Scouring rush.	Niya'wibûkûk'	Boneset.
Gi'jikan'dûg	Arbor vitæ.	Nokwe'jigûn	White mugwort.
Gine'bigwûck	Plantain.	O'ckinigi'kweäni'bĭc	Tansy.
Ginoje'wûkûn	Yellow dock.	Oda'tagago'mĭnaga'wûnj	Blackberry (also black raspberry).
Gĭ'tciode'imĭnĭdji'bĭk	Five-finger.		
Gi'zĭso'bûgons'	Ox-eye, psoralea, cone flower.	Ode'imĭnĭdji'bĭk	Wild strawberry.
		Odiga'dimanido'	New Jersey tea.
Gi'zĭso'mûcki'ki	Goldenrod.	Odji'bĭkĕns	Goldenrod.
Gi'zûswe'bigwa'nĭs	Cone flower.	Odji'biknamûn'	Puccoon.
Gogeda'djibûg	Pasque flower.	Odjici'gomĭn	Wild lettuce.
Gûzigwa'komĭnaga'wûnj	Shadbush.	O'gima'wûck	Mugwort.
Ĭ'ckode'bûg	Mugwort.	Ogĭni'mĭnaga'wûnj	Rose (term refers to the rose-berry).
Ĭ'ckode'wadji'bĭk	Shepherd's purse.		
Ikwe'mĭc	Wild cherry.	O'gite'bûg	Cowslip.
Inĭ'nĭwûnj	Common milkweed.	Ogwis'simaûn'	Pumpkin.
Inĭ'nĭwĭn'dĭbĭge'gûn	Wake-robin.	Oja'cidji'bĭk	Fireweed.
Jĭngwak'	Red pine, white pine.	Ojig'imĭn'	Smartweed.
Jĭn'gwakwan'dûg	Mugwort.	O'mûkiki'bûg	Plantain.
Jo'mĭnaga'wûnj	Grape.	O'mûkiki'wida'sûn	Pitcher-plant.
Maĭn'gamûna'tĭg	Snowberry.	O'mûcko'zowa'no	Elk tail.
Ma'kibûg	Sumac.	O'saga'tigom	Sweet cicely.
Ma'kodji'bĭk	Carrion flower.	O'zawa'bigwûn	Wormseed, mustard, goldenrod.
Ma'kwona'gĭc obji'bĭk	Dogbane.		
Ma'nanons'	Hop hornbeam.	Oza'widji'bĭk	Goldthread, bitter dock, yellow dock.
Man'asa'dĭ	Balsam poplar.		
Manda'mĭn	Corn.	Ozĭ'sĭgo'bimĭc	Willow.
Manido'bima'kwûd	Woodbine.	Saga'komĭn'agûnj'	Bearberry.
Mano'mĭn	Wild rice.	Sasa'bikwan	Dogbane.
Ma'zana'tĭg	Nettle, thistle.	Siga'gawûnj'	Wild leek.
Me'skwana'kûk	Joe-Pye-weed.	Wadûb'	Alder.
Micidji'mĭnaga'wûnj	Wild currant.	Wa'bigwûn'	Pearly everlasting (and other plants).
Mi'gĭsĕns'Ĭbûg	False gromwell.		
Mĭnaga'wûnj	Blueberry.	Wabino'wûck	Horsemint.
Mĭne'saga'wûnj	Thornapple.	Wabos'odji'bĭk	Wild sarsaparilla (also wild currant).
Mĭ'nĭsĭno'wûck	Wild pea.		
Mĭs'kodji'bĭk	Bloodroot.	Wabos'obûgons'	Creeping snowberry.
Mĭs'kwabi'mĭc	Red-osier dogwood.	Weza'wûnûckwûk'	Giant hyssop.
Mĭs'komĭnaga'wûnj	Red raspberry.	Wicko'bimûcko'si	Sweetgrass.
Miskwa'wak	Red cedar.	Wi'cosidji'bĭk	Red baneberry.
Mĭtĭgo'mĭc	Bur oak.	Wigub'imĭj	Basswood.
Mĭtĭgo'mizĭnc	Oak.	Wi'gwasa'tĭg	White birch.
Mĭ'tĭgwabak'	Hickory.	Wikĕn'	Calamus.
Mŭckig'obûg	Labrador tea.	Wĭnabojo'bikwûk'	Lily.
Mŭ'ckigwa'tĭg	Tamarack.		

LIST OF PLANTS ARRANGED ACCORDING TO NATIVE NAME—Continued

Native name	Common name	Native name	Common name
Wĭnabojo′ noko′mĭs wi′nĭzĭsûn′.	Painted-cup.	Wi′sûgibûg′	Burdock.
		Wi′sûgi′mĭtĭgo′mĭc	Bitter oak.
Wi′nibĭdja′bibaga′no	Chickweed.	Wi′sûgidji′bĭk	Culver's root.
Wĭnĭ′sĭbûgons′	Wintergreen.	Ze′sûb	False nettle.
Wĭnĭ′sĭkĕns	Aster.	Zi′gĭnĭ′ce	Harebell.

An investigation was made to determine whether the plants used medicinally by the Chippewa have a recognized use by the white race. Two reports on this subject were courteously prepared by Dr. W. W. Stockberger, physiologist in charge of drug, poisonous and oil plant investigations, Bureau of Plant Industry, United States Department of Agriculture. The first report shows the medicinal properties of such plants and the second report shows the principal active medicinal constituents of these plants.

MEDICINAL PROPERTIES OF PLANTS USED BY THE CHIPPEWA

The following 69 plants used by the Chippewa are regarded as medicinal by white people, although opinion as to their therapeutic value varies greatly. The few species now officially recognized in the latest editions of the United States Pharmacopoeia and the National Formulary are designated in the text by the abbreviations U. S. P. IX and N. F. 4, respectively. Species recognized in the eighth revision of the United States Pharmacopoeia but no longer official are indicated by U. S. P. VIII.

The remaining species, some of which were recognized in the earlier Pharmacopoeias, have long been used either in medicine as practiced by certain physicians or as domestic remedies.

Abies balsamea (L.) Mill. Balsam. PINACEAE. Pine family.

Canada balsam, a liquid oleoresin obtained from this tree, is stimulant, diuretic, occasionally diaphoretic and externally rubefacient. U. S. P. VIII.

Achillea millefolium L. Yarrow, Milfoil. COMPOSITAE. Composite family.

The plant is slightly astringent and has been used as an alterative, diuretic, and as a stimulant tonic.

Acorus calamus L. Sweetflag, calamus. ARACEAE. Arum family.

The rhizome has been employed as an aromatic stimulant and tonic. U. S. P. VIII.

Actaea rubra (Ait.) Willd. Red baneberry. RANUNCULACEAE. Crowfoot family.

The rhizome is said to be emeto-purgative and parasiticide.

Alnus incana (L.) Moench. Speckled alder. FAGACEAE. Beech family.

The bark is alterative, astringent, and emetic.

Apocynum androsaemifolium L. Spreading dogbane. APOCYNACEAE. Dogbane family.

The root is diuretic, sudorific, emetic, cathartic, and anthelmintic. U. S. P. VIII.

Aralia nudicaulis L. Wild sarsaparilla. ARALIACEAE. Ginseng family.

The roots have been used for their gently stimulant, diaphoretic, and alterative action.

Aralia racemosa L. Spikenard. ARALIACEAE. Ginseng family.

The root is alterative, stimulant, and diaphoretic.

Arctium minus Bernh. Burdock. COMPOSITAE. Composite family.

The root is diuretic, diaphoretic, and alterative. U. S. P. VIII.

Arctostaphylos uva-ursi (L.) Spreng. Bearberry. ERICACEAE. Heath family.

The leaves have mild and slightly antiseptic diuretic properties. U. S. P. IX.

Arisaema triphyllum (L.) Torr. Jack-in-the-pulpit. ARACEAE. Arum family.

Mentioned in unofficial part of United States and King's Dispensatories.

Artemisia absinthium L. Wormwood. COMPOSITAE. Composite family.

The leaves and flowering tops are tonic, stomachic, stimulant, febrifuge, and anthelmintic.

Artemisia dracunculoides Pursh. Fuzzy-weed. COMPOSITAE. Composite family.

The plant acts as a topical irritant and diaphoretic.

Asarum canadense L. Wild ginger. ARISTOLOCHIACEAE. Birthwort family.

The rhizome and roots are used as a carminative agent and flavor. N. F. 4.

Asclepias incarnata L. Swamp milkweed. ASCLEPIADACEAE. Milkweed family.

The root is alterative, anthelmintic, cathartic, and emetic.

Asclepias syriaca L. Milkweed. ASCLEPIADACEAE. Milkweed family.

The root is tonic, diuretic, alterative, emmenagogue, purgative, and emetic.

Athyrium filix-foemina (L.) Roth. Lady fern. POLYPODIACEAE. Fern family.

Reputed taenicide and formerly so used.

Bursa bursa-pastoris (L.) Britton. Shepherd's Purse. CRUCIFERAE. Mustard family.

This plant was formerly thought to be antiscorbutic.

Caltha palustris L. Marsh marigold. RANUNCULACEAE. Crowfoot family.

The plant has been popularly used in the treatment of coughs.

Caulophyllum thalictroides (L.) Michx. Blue Cohosh. BERBERIDACEAE. Barbery family.

The rhizome and roots are said to be sedative, diuretic, and emmenagogue. N. F. 4.

Celastrus scandens L. Bittersweet. CELASTRACEAE. Staff tree family.

The bark is said to be emetic, diaphoretic, and alterative.

Cirsium sp. COMPOSITAE. Composite family.

The related species *Cirsium arvense* is said to be tonic, diuretic, and astringent.

Cornus alternifolia L. f. Blue or purple dogwood. CORNACEAE. Dogwood family.

The bark of the root of the related species, *Cornus florida*, is a feeble, astringent tonic.

Cypripedium hirsutum Mill. Showy ladyslipper. ORCHIDACEAE. Orchis family.

The rhizome and roots have been described as tonic, stimulant, and diaphoretic. N. F. 4.

Dirca palustris L. Wicopy. THYMELAEACEAE. Mezereum family.

The berries are said to be narcotic and poisonous. The bark is purgative and emetic and when fresh vesicant.

Epilobium angustifolium L. Great willow-herb. ONAGRACEAE. Evening primrose family.

The plant is tonic, astringent, demulcent, and emollient.

Erigeron canadensis L. Horseweed. COMPOSITAE. Composite family.

The plant is diuretic, tonic, and astringent.

Eupatorium maculatum L. Spotted boneset. COMPOSITAE. Composite family.

The dried leaves and flowering tops are used to prepare a domestic diaphoretic tea. N. F. 4.

Fragaria virginiana Duchesne. Wild strawberry. ROSACEAE. Rose family.

The leaves are slightly astringent; the roots diuretic.

Gaultheria procumbens L. Wintergreen, Checkerberry. ERICACEAE. Heath family.

The leaves are aromatic and astringent.

Geranium maculatum L. Cranesbill. GERANIACEAE. Geranium family.

The rhizome is an absolute intestinal astringent. N. F. 4.

Heracleum lanatum Michx. Cow parsnip, beaver root. UMBELLIFERAE. Parsley family.

The leaves and roots are rubefacient; the root is said to be carminative and stimulant.

Koellia virginiana (L.) MacM. Virginia thyme. LABIATAE. Mint family.

The plant is diaphoretic, carminative, and tonic.

Lactuca canadensis L. Wild lettuce. COMPOSITAE. Composite family.

The juice of the plant is said to be mildly narcotic.

Larix laricina (DuRoi) Koch. Tamarack. PINACEAE. Pine family.

The bark is said to be laxative, tonic, diuretic, and alterative.

Ledum groenlandicum Oeder. Labrador tea. ERICACEAE. Heath family.

The leaves are expectorant and tonic. They are said to have been employed instead of tea leaves during the Revolutionary War.

Leptandra virginica (L.) Nutt. Culver's-root. SCROPHULARIACEAE. Figwort family.

The rhizome and roots are alterative, cholagogue, and cathartic. N. F. 4.

Nepeta cataria L. Catnip. LABIATAE. Mint family.

The leaves and flowering tops have long had a domestic use as a mild stimulant and tonic and as an emmenagogue.

Nymphaea americana (Prov.) Miller & Standley. Pondlily. NYMPHAEACEAE. Waterlily family.

The rhizome of the closely related species *Nymphaea advena* is astringent and demulcent.

Osmorrhiza claytoni (Michx.) Clarke. Sweet cicely. UMBELLIFERAE. Parsley family.

The root of the closely related *Osmorrhiza longistylis* is aromatic, carminative, and stomachic.

Ostrya virginiana (Mill.) Koch. American hop hornbeam. BETULACEAE. Birch family.

The bark and inner wood are antiperiodic, tonic, and alterative.

Plantago major L. Large plantain. PLANTAGINACEAE. Plantain family.
The roots and leaves are alterative, diuretic, and antiseptic.

Populus balsamifera L. Balsam poplar. SALICACEAE. Willow family.
The leaf buds are resinous, aromatic, and expectorant.

Populus tremuloides Michx. American aspen. SALICACEAE. Willow family.
The bark is tonic and febrifuge.

Potentilla palustris (L.) Scop. Marsh five-finger. ROSACEAE. Rose family.
The roots are bitter and astringent, but do not appear to have been used in medicine.

Prunus serotina Ehrh. Wild black cherry. ROSACEAE. Rose family.
The dried bark is tonic, sedative, pectoral, and astringent. U. S. P. IX.

Prunus virginiana L. Chokecherry. ROSACEAE. Rose family.
The fruit is very astringent.

Psoralea argophylla Pursh. LEGUMINOSAE. Pea family.
The root and leaves of several species of *Psoralea* appear to possess the properties of a mild, stimulating, bitter tonic.

Pulsatilla hirsutissima (Pursh) Britton Pasque flower. RANUNCULACEAE. Crowfoot family.
The plant has been recommended as an alterative, sedative, and antispasmodic. N. F. 4.

Quercus rubra L. Red oak. FAGACEAE. Beech family.
Oak bark is slightly tonic, powerfully astringent and antiseptic.

Rhus glabra L. Smooth sumac. ANACARDIACEAE. Cashew family.
The dried ripe fruits are astringent and refrigerant. N. F. 4.

Rubus strigosus Michx. Wild red raspberry. ROSACEAE. Rose family.
The juice of the ripe fruits is used for flavoring. N. F. 4.

Rudbeckia laciniata L. COMPOSITAE. Composite family.
The herb is said to be diuretic, tonic, and balsamic.

Rumex crispus L. Yellow dock. POLYGONACEAE. Buckwheat family.
The root is astringent, slightly tonic and has been supposed to have alterative properties. N. F. 4.

Sanguinaria canadensis L. Bloodroot. PAPAVERACEAE. Poppy family.
The rhizome and roots are irritant and narcotic, expectorant in small doses, but in large doses nauseant and emetic. U. S. P. IX.

Sanicula canadensis L. Black snakeroot. UMBELLIFERAE. Parsley family.
The root is said to be astringent, antispasmodic, and antiperiodic.

Silphium perfoliatum L. Cup-plant. COMPOSITAE. Composite family.
The plant is tonic, diaphoretic, and diuretic.

Solidago rigida L. Goldenrod. COMPOSITAE. Composite family.
The herb is astringent and styptic.

Solidago rigidiuscula Porter. Goldenrod: COMPOSITAE. Composite family.
Supposed to have properties similar to the preceding species.

Stachys palustris L. Woundwort. LABIATAE. Mint family.
The herb is said to be expectorant and vulnerary.

Stellaria media (L.) Cyrill. Common chickweed. CARYOPHYLLACEAE. Pink family.
The leaves appear to be a cooling demulcent.

Symphoricarpos albus (L.) Blake. Snowberry. CAPRIFOLIACEAE. Honeysuckle
family.
The root is alterative and tonic.

Tanacetum vulgare L. Tansy. COMPOSITAE. Composite family.
The leaves and tops are tonic, emmenagogue and diaphoretic.

Taraxacum officinale Weber. Dandelion. COMPOSITAE. Composite family.
The rhizome and roots are used as a bitter tonic and as a mild laxative.
U. S. P. IX.

Thuja occidentalis L. Arborvitae. PINACEAE. Pine family.
An extract prepared from the leafy young twigs has been recommended as a
febrifuge, expectorant, and anthelmintic. N. F. 4.

Trillium grandiflorum (Michx.) Salisb. LILIACEAE. Lily family.
The rhizome has been used as an astringent and tonic expectorant.

Tsuga canadensis (L.) Carr. Hemlock. PINACEAE. Pine family.
Canada pitch obtained from this tree is a gentle rubefacient.

Urtica gracilis Ait. Nettle. URTICACEAE. Nettle family.
Several related species of nettle have been used in medicine as local irritants
and as diuretics.

Viburnum acerifolium L. Arrow-wood. CAPRIFOLIACEAE. Honeysuckle family.
The bark was formerly used as an astringent.

Zanthoxylum americanum Mill. Prickly ash. RUTACEAE. Rue family.
The bark is sialagogue, stimulant, alterative, and emetic. U. S. P. IX.

PRINCIPAL ACTIVE MEDICINAL CONSTITUENTS OF PLANTS USED BY THE CHIPPEWA

Abies balsamea. Constituents: A true turpentine consisting of 24 parts essential oil and 60 parts resin. By fractional distillation the oil has been resolved
into bornyl or terpinyl acetate, pinene, and a fragrant oil resembling oil of
lemon.

Achillea millefolium. Constituents: A blue volatile oil containing cineol and a
bitter principle, achillein.

Acorus calamus. Constituents: The rhizome yields a volatile oil which has the
composition of a terpene.

Actaea rubra. Constituents: Two resins which have a physiological action
resembling that of the active principles of *Cimicifuga* and *Helleborus*.

Alnus incana. Constituents: Tannin, volatile oil, and resins.

Apocynum androsaemifolium. Constituents: Resins, caoutchouc, a volatile oil,
and a bitter principle consisting of the glucosides apocynamarin, apocynein,
androsin, and the glyceride androsterin.

Aralia nudicaulis. Constituents: An acrid resin, and araliin, a yellowish
glucoside.

Aralia racemosa. Constituents: Same as *A. nudicaulis.*

Arctium minus. Constituents: Inulin, sugar, volatile oil, and a bitter glucoside.

Arctostaphylos uva-ursi. Constituents: Tannic acid, gallic acid, gum, resin,
urson, arbutin, and ericolin.

Artemisia absinthium. Constituents: A volatile oil and absinthin, a bitter
principle.

Artemisia dracunculoides. Constituents: (?)

Asarum canadense. Constituents: A phenol $C_9H_{12}O_2$, pinene, a blue oil, a lactone,
palmitic acid, acetic acid, and a mixture of fatty acids and oleoresin.

Asclepias incarnata. Constituents: A volatile oil, resins, and the glucoside asclepiadin.

Asclepias syriaca. Constituents: Similar to those of *A. incarnata* and in addition asclepion.

Athyrium filix-foemina. Constituents: The active principle resembles filicic acid.

Bursa bursa-pastoris. Constituents: A volatile oil identical with that of mustard, and the alkaloid bursine.

Caltha palustris. Constituents: Berberin and an alkaloid similar to nicotine.

Caulophyllum thalictroides. Constituents: Resins, a substance similar to saponin, and the glucoside leontin.

Celastrus scandens. Constituents: A volatile oil and celastrin.

Cirsium arvense. Constituents: A volatile alkaloid and the glucoside cnicin.

Cornus alternifolia. Constituents: Cornine.

Cypripedium hirsutum. Constituents: A volatile oil and the glucosidal resinoid, cypripedin.

Diervilla lonicera. Constituents: Alkaloid believed to be narceine; a glucoside similar to fraxina in *D. lutea.*

Dirca palustris. Constituents: Undetermined.

Epilobium augustifolium. Constituents: Undetermined.

Erigeron canadensis. Constituents: A volatile oil.

Eupatorium maculatum. Constituents: Undetermined.

Fragaria virginiana. Constituents: The glucoside fragarianin.

Gaultheria procumbens. Constituents: A volatile oil containing the terpene gaultherilene and methyl salicylate.

Geranium maculatum. Constituents: Tannin.

Heracleum lanatum. Constituents: A volatile oil.

Koellia virginiana. Constituents: (?)

Lactuca canadensis. Constituents: The bitter principle lactucin, lactucic acid, lactucopicrin, lactucerin, and a volatile oil.

Larix laricina. Constituents: A volatile oil which contains pinene, larixine, and the ester bornylacetate.

Ledum groenlandicum. Constituents: The glucoside ericolin.

Leptandra virginica. Constituents: The glucoside leptandrin.

Nepeta cataria. Constituents: A volatile oil.

Nymphaea americana. Constituents: Undetermined.

Osmorrhiza claytoni. The related species *O. longistylis* yields a volatile oil composed chiefly of anethol.

Ostrya virginiana. Constituents: Undetermined.

Plantago major. Constituents: Not well known.

Populus balsamifera. Constituents: Chrysin, tetrochrysin, salicin, populin, resin and a volatile oil.

Populus tremuloides. Constituents: See *P. balsamifera.*

Potentilla palustris. Constituents: A bitter principle, mucilage and tannins.

Prunus serotina. Constituents: A glucoside.

Prunus virginiana. Constituents: A glucoside.

Psoralea argophylla. Constituents: (?)

Pulsatilla hirsutissima. Constituents: A volatile oil containing a camphor.

Quercus rubra. Constituents: Tannic acid, a terpene, resin and quercitrin.

Rhus glabra. Constituents: Tannic acid and gallic acid.

Rubus strigosus. Constituents of fruit: Citric and malic acids.

Rudbeckia laciniata. Constituents: (?)

Rumex crispus. Constituents: Tannin, albumen and iron.

Sanguinaria canadensis. Constituents: The alkaloid chelerythrine, sanguina-rine, gamma-homochelidonine and protopine.

Sanicula canadensis. Constituents: A resin and an essential oil.

Silphium perfoliatum. Constituents: Undetermined.

Solidago rigida. Constituents: A volatile oil.

Solidago rigidiuscula. Constituents: A volatile oil.

Stachys palustris. Constituents: An aromatic substance and an alkaloid.

Stellaria media. Constituents: Saponin.

Symphoricarpos albus. Constituents: Invertin, a glucoside and emulsin.

Tanacetum vulgare. Constituents: The bitter principle tanacetin and a vola-tile oil.

Taraxacum officinale. Constituents: The bitter principles taraxicin taraxa-cerin.

Thuja occidentalis. Constituents: The coloring matter thujin, the glucoside, penipicrin, and a volatile oil containing dutro-pinene, laevo-fenchone and dextro-thujone.

Trillium grandiflorum. Constituents: Undetermined.

Tsuga canadensis. Constituents: Resin and a volatile oil which contains laevo-pinene and laevo-bornylacetate.

Urtica gracilis. Constituents: A volatile oil.

Viburnum acerifolium. Constituents: Probably viburnin and valerianic acid.

Zanthoxylum americanum. Constituents: Zanthoxylin and an alkaloid resem-bling berberine.

PLANTS AS FOOD

The strength of the Chippewa in conquering the Sioux and establishing themselves in new territory indicates that they were well nourished, that suitable food was available, and that it was prepared in a proper manner. This was the work of the women, who were very industrious and bestowed much care on the provisioning of their households. A staple article of food was wild rice, which was seasoned with maple sugar or combined with broth made from ducks or venison. An important food value was obtained from maple sugar. Fish were extensively used, as the Chippewa, lacking horses, lived along the lakes and watercourses as much as possible. It is said that they had squash and pumpkins before the coming of the white man, and the country abounded in berries and wild fruit of many varieties. Thus it is seen that the Chippewa were a people subsisting chiefly on vegetable products and fish, though they secured deer and other animals by hunting. The making of gardens was an important phase of the industrial year, and a portion of the food thus obtained was stored in caches for winter use.

While the present chapter concerns the use of vegetable foods it may be added that fish were stored by drying and by freezing; and that meat was dried, after which it usually was pounded and mixed with tallow for storage. The Chippewa cooked and ate all trapped animals except the marten. Rabbits were caught in snares and formed a valuable food during the winter months. Deer and moose were available, and bear meat was liked because it was so fat. The bear was an especially useful animal, as all parts of it were either eaten or utilized.

LIST OF PLANTS USED AS FOOD

Botanical name	Common name	Part of plant used
Acer saccharum Marsh_____	Maple_____	Sap.
Amelanchier canadensis (L.) Medic___	Juneberry_____	Fruit.
Arctostaphylos uva-ursi (L.) Spreng__	Bearberry_____	Fruit.
Asarum canadense L_____	Wild ginger_____	Root.
Asclepias syriaca L_____	Common milkweed__	Flowers.
Aster species_____	Aster_____	Leaves.
Chiogenes hispidula (L.) T. & G_____	Creeping snowberry__	Leaves.
Cornus canadensis L_____	_____	Fruit.
Corylus americana Walt_____	Hazel_____	Nut.
Crataegus species_____	Thornapple_____	Fruit.
Cucurbita maxima Duchesne_____	Squash_____	Fruit.
Cucurbita pepo L_____	Pumpkin_____	Fruit.
Falcata comosa (L.) Kuntze_____	Wild bean or "Hog peanut."	Root.
Fragaria virginiana Duchesne_____	Strawberry_____	Fruit.
Gaultheria procumbens L _____	Wintergreen_____	Leaves.
Helianthus tuberosus L_____	Jerusalem artichoke__	Root.
Koellia virginiana (L.) MacM_____	Mountain mint_____	Flowers and buds.
Ledum groenlandicum Oeder_____	Labrador tea_____	Leaves.
Lycopus asper Greene_____	Bugleweed _____	Root.
Oxycoccus macrocarpus (Ait.) Pers___	Cranberry_____	Fruit.
Parthenocissus quinquefolia (L.) Greene.	Woodbine (Virginia creeper).	Stalk and sap next the bark.
Populus tremuloides Michx_____	Poplar_____	Sap.
Prunus americana Marsh_____	Chokecherry_____	Twigs.
Prunus serotina Ehrh_____	Wild cherry_____	Twigs.
Prunus virginiana L_____	Chokecherry_____	Twigs.
Quercus macrocarpa Muhl_____	Bur oak_____	Fruit (acorns).
Ribes triste Pall_____	Red currant _____	Fruit.
Ribes species_____	Wild currant_____	Fruit.
Rubus frondosus Bigel. (?) _____	Blackberry _____	Fruit.
Rubus strigosus Michx_____	Red raspberry_____	Fruit.
Sagittaria latifolia Vahl_____	Arrowhead_____	Root.
Scirpus validus Vahl_____	Bulrush_____	Root.
Tilia americana L_____	Basswood_____	Sap next the bark.
Tsuga canadensis (L.) Carr_____	Hemlock_____	Leaves.
Vaccinium angustifolium Ait_____	Blueberry _____	Fruit.
Viburnum pauciflorum Pylaie_____	Highland cranberry _	Fruit.
Vitis cordifolia Michx_____	Grape_____	Fruit.
Zea mays L _____	Corn_____	Fruit.
Zizania palustris L_____	Indian rice_____	Fruit.

MAKING MAPLE SUGAR [2]

The two most important vegetable foods were maple sugar and wild rice. The obtaining of these commodities was attended with much pleasure, though the temporary camps were busy and there was work for young and old. Each family or group of two or three families had its own sugar bush, as it also had its own part of the rice field, and the people went there in the early spring to make the year's supply of sugar. Two structures remained in the sugar camp from year to year. These were the birch-bark lodge in which the utensils were stored, and the frame of the lodge in which the sugar was made. (Pl. 31.) The former was generally round in shape, but the one visited by the writer was constructed with a "ridge pole" to give more room at the top. The latter was made in a substantial manner and consisted of a stout framework of poles covered with sheets of elm or cedar bark. Rolls of birch bark might, if desired, be substituted for the heavier bark on the roof. The size of the lodge varied with the number of families in the camp. The lodge visited by the writer was of average size, the length being 18½ feet, the width 19 feet 3 inches, and the height at the eaves 10 feet. There was an entrance at each end and a platform extended the entire length at each side. These platforms were about 5 feet wide, 12 to 18 inches high, and might be on one or both sides of the lodge. They were intended primarily for sleeping, but the edge next the fire was used for sitting and eating, after the bedding had been rolled and placed next to the walls of the lodge. If possible, the platform on one side was reserved for the sugar-making utensils. In a small lodge the platform might be on only one side, the utensils being placed on the ground at the opposite side of the lodge.

The fire space extended the length of the lodge beneath the ridge of the roof, and a large log of green wood was placed at each side of it. A structure for holding the kettles was erected above the fire space. This structure consisted of four heavy corner posts, 6 or 7 feet high, with crotches at the top. Between the crotches of the posts, crosswise of the lodge, were laid stout poles, upon which were poles laid lengthwise, and between these, over the fire, were placed the horizontal bars from which the kettles were suspended. Thus it was possible by moving the horizontal bars to place a kettle over any part of the fire. The largest kettles were hung in the center

---

[2] It is said that "the primitive Indian method of making sugar before the introduction of metal kettles was to throw red-hot stones in vessels of bark or wood, or again, to freeze the syrup repeatedly in shallow basins and throw off the ice." Dr. V. Havard, U. S. A., "Drink plants of the North American Indians," Bulletin of the Torrey Botanical Club, Lancaster, Pa., 1896, vol. 23, no. 2, pp. 42–43.

a, CASS LAKE, MINN.

b, STREAM, WHITE EARTH. MINN.

FRAME OF LODGE IN WHICH MAPLE SAP WAS BOILED, AND STORAGE LODGE FOR UTENSILS (CLOSED)

a, STORAGE LODGE (OPEN)

b, BIRCH-BARK CONTAINERS

c, BIRCH-BARK CONE, DISH, AND SPOONS

a, BOILING MAPLE SAP

b, MAPLE TREES TAPPED

of the lodge. They were suspended by strips of green bark, later by chains and iron hooks made by blacksmiths. The smaller kettles were placed over the ends of the fire, and usually were hung on wooden hooks made of tree crotches, ironwood being frequently used for this purpose.

To add to the comfort of the lodge, a double shelf was fastened to the side of the framework for holding small articles. This was placed near the door, where it could conveniently be reached by the mistress of the lodge.

The capacity or size of a sugar bush was not estimated by the number of maple trees but by the number of "taps," as it was not unusual to make two or three taps in a large tree. Nine hundred taps was an average size. The number of taps was reckoned by hundreds, the larger camps being mentioned as having 1,200 or 2,000 taps.

The season of sugar making began about the middle of March and lasted about a month. It is said that the best sugar was made when the early part of the winter had been open, allowing the ground to freeze deeper than usual, this being followed by deep snow. The first run of sap was considered the best. A storm usually followed the first warm weather, and afterwards the sap began to flow again. This sap, however, grained less easily than the first and had a slightly different flavor. Rain produced a change in the taste and a thunderstorm is said to have destroyed the characteristic flavor of the sugar.

The procedure of moving to the sugar camp depended somewhat upon the condition of the lodge. If repairs with sheets of heavy bark were needed, it was customary for the men to go early to the camp. The following account presupposes a lodge with birch-bark rolls as its roof covering. If such a lodge were in use the women went first to the camp, making their way on snowshoes through the forest. On their backs they carried the rolls of birch bark for the roof covering. These rolls were carried perpendicularly by a pack strap across the forehead. They were not heavy, but towered high above a woman's head.

Arriving at the camp, the women shoveled the snow away from the sugar lodge and soon made themselves comfortable. A ladder of tree branches was among the articles stored during the winter, and placing this against the framework of the lodge they ascended and spread their rolls of birch bark on the roof. On the platforms in the interior of the lodge they spread cedar boughs, if such were available, and on these were laid rush mats, over which were spread blankets and warm furs. The storehouse was opened, the great rolls of birch bark being turned back, one at a time, until beneath the weather-worn coverings were seen the heaps of bark dishes, makuks, and buckets, white outside and warm yellow within, others a soft gray or dulled by age to a rich mahogany color. (Pl. 32, a.) The odor of balsam and dry sweet birch bark came from the lodge. There was also a supply of birch bark for making new utensils (pl. 32, *b*, *c*), if such were necessary. The material which the women brought with them from the winter camps depended, of course, on their knowledge of what had been left in the storing lodge the previous season.

Having opened this lodge, the women examined the utensils. The bark dishes for gathering sap were tied in bundles of 10 and placed upside down when stored. They were about 12 inches long. There were the makuks in which the sugar was stored, and utensils somewhat similar in shape, but provided with handles, thus resembling buckets. In these the sap was carried to the sugar lodge. The makuk varied in size from those holding a small quantity of sugar to those holding 100 pounds or more. Although birch bark was plentiful it was not wasted. Bark utensils were washed and dried at the close of each sugar making, and with this care could be used 5 or even 10 years. The women looked them over and mended with balsam gum any that needed repairing. The color of the sugar depended on the whiteness and cleanness of the utensils. They also made new utensils if necessary, using the supply of bark left in the lodge for that purpose. In addition to the birch-bark utensils there were troughs made of logs, basswood being commonly used for that purpose. Outside one or both entrances to the sugar lodge there was such a trough, into which the sap was poured from buckets. Some of these troughs would hold several barrels of sap. They were covered with sheets of birch bark to keep out twigs and bits of moss. A trough was also used in the process of granulating the sugar. Certain utensils were commonly made of maple, among these being the large wooden spoons used in dipping the sap, the paddles with which the sirup was stirred, and the granulating ladles with the back of which the heavy sirup was worked into sugar.

When all arrangements were completed the women returned to the camp and prepared for the removal of their families and household equipment. These were carried on either toboggans or sleds, drawn usually by dogs. Among the articles that were not stored but carried each year to the camps were the large brass kettles for boiling the sap. Small children or members of the family too feeble to walk were placed comfortably on the sledges among the packs. The women carried the smallest children on their backs, and the party started for the annual sugar making.

On arriving at the sugar camp it was sometimes necessary to erect a tipi for temporary use, while the men repaired the structure for holding the kettles. Great care was taken to have this in perfect condition, as the fall of a kettle would be a serious accident in a lodge. The tapping of the trees was begun as soon as the people took up their abode in the sugar lodge, provided the sap was running at that time. Tapping was done only by those who were expert in the use of an ax, though women as well as men engaged in the task. (Pl. 33, b.) The trees were arranged in paths so that the collecting of the sap could be conveniently done. A good worker could make 300 tappings in a day. The tapping consisted in making a diagonal cut in a tree about 3½ inches long and about 3 feet from the ground. Below the lower end of this cut the bark was removed in a perpendicular line for a distance of about 4 inches. A wooden spile was inserted below this point. The wooden spiles were commonly made of slippery elm and were about 6 inches long, 2 inches wide, and curved on the under surface. The distance of a spile below the cut in a maple tree depended on the grain and hardness of the wood. If it were inserted too near the cut there was danger that the wood might split. The cut in which the spile was inserted could be made with an ax, or with a tool resembling a curved chisel, which was pounded into the tree and removed for the insertion of the wooden spile.

The sap dishes were distributed in the early morning, being placed on the ground or the snow beneath the taps. If the weather were cold the sap did not run during the night, and accordingly in the late afternoon when it stopped running the people began to gather it, pouring from the dishes into bark pails carried by the women, or large buckets carried by the men. In the very large camps it was sometimes necessary to have barrels stationed at a distance from the sugar lodge, and to fill them and haul them on sleds. A shoulder yoke enabling a man to carry two buckets was used among the Chippewa to some extent, but it is said that the use of the yoke was learned from the French, and did not represent a native custom.

When the sap was taken to the camp it was put into the kettles or poured into the troughs at the doors. The large kettles were at first filled only partially, the sap being heated in the smaller kettles near the ends of the fire and emptied from these into the large kettles, in which the actual boiling was done. By this means the entire quantity of sap was heated gradually. (Pl. 33, a.)

All night the fires were kept burning and the kettles boiling, certain people taking turns in watching them. If a kettle boiled too rapidly a branch of spruce attached to a stick was dipped into the froth. The motion was little more than a brushing of the froth with the spruce, but the bubbling at once subsided. By early morning the sirup was slightly thickened and ready to strain. In the old days a mat woven of narrow strips of basswood bark was placed over an extra kettle, and the sirup was strained through this mat, being dipped from the kettle with large wooden spoons. In more recent times the sirup is slowly strained through a burlap, and it is said that a clean threadbare white blanket was occasionally used for this purpose. Straining completed this stage of the process of sugar making.

The "sugaring off" was postponed until a day when there was a storm, or when the sap boiling was discontinued.

Before replacing the sap in the kettles they were thoroughly cleaned, bunches of stiff rushes which commonly grow near sugar bush being used, and the kettles polished with them. All the utensils were washed and everything made ready for the final process, which required special care. The sirup was replaced in the kettles and slowly heated. When it became thick, small pieces of deer tallow were put in it. This was said to make the sugar soft and not brittle. A maple-wood paddle was used in stirring the sirup, and when it had thickened to the proper consistency it was quickly transferred to the granulating trough, where it was again stirred with a paddle, and at the proper time "rubbed or worked" with the back of the granulating ladle, or in some instances pulverized by hand. This had to be done very rapidly before the sugar cooled too much. The stirring of the thick sirup and the granulating was a heavy task, and it was not unusual for men to assist in the work. From the granulating trough the warm sugar was poured into makuks. (Pl. 34.)

Granulated sugar, however, was not the only form into which maple sap was converted. When the reboiling for sugar was begun it was customary to pour some of the thick sirup into small containers where it hardened solidly. (Pl. 35.) Little cones were made of birch bark and fastened together with strips of basswood bark so that the group resembled a cluster of berries. These cones filled with sugar were a favorite delicacy among the children. The upper mandible of a duckbill was similarly filled, several of these being fastened together in a row by a little stick. Little birch-bark dishes of the shape commonly used for all purposes were also filled, and sugar cakes were made in fancy shapes, the molds being cut from soft wood and greased before the sirup was put into them so that it could easily be taken out. These molds were in shape of various animals, also of men, and of the moon and stars, originality of design being sought. A product called gum sugar was highly prized. This was a sticky substance and was kept in packets of birch bark tied with basswood bark. In making the latter delicacy the sirup was taken from the kettle just before it was ready to grain. It was then poured on snow and not stirred. When cold it was placed in the birch-bark wrapping.

As already stated, the last run of sap had a different taste than the first and grained less easily. This was boiled as thickly as possible and placed in makuks. Sometimes these makuks were buried in the ground and covered with bark and boughs to keep the contents cool during the summer so that it would neither become sour nor freeze. Makuks of this substance were often placed in the storing lodge of a sugar camp where the women could get them at any time. If left an entire year, the women, on returning to the sugar camp, found it as fresh as when placed in storage.

The uses of maple sugar were many and varied. It was used in seasoning fruits, vegetables, cereals, and fish. It was dissolved in water as a cooling summer drink and sometimes made into sirup in which medicine was boiled for children. The granulated sugar and the sugar cakes were commonly used as gifts, and a woman with a goodly supply of maple sugar in its various forms was regarded as a thrifty woman providing for the wants of her family.

A pleasing diversion of the young people was the making of birch-bark transparencies, described on pages 390–396.

A Chippewa living in Canada where there are few maple trees said that his people tap the white birch trees and boil the sap into sirup. He said that the sap of these trees does not run as long as maple sap.

Gathering Wild Rice

Wild rice constitutes the chief cereal food of the Chippewa. It abounds in certain lakes, ripening earliest in the shallow lakes fed by streams and later in the lakes fed by springs. The soil of some lakes seems to produce more rice and larger kernels than that of other lakes. By a wise provision of nature the seed of the rice is carried by wild ducks, which also afford food for the people at the season when the rice is ripe.

In the old days each family or small group of families had a portion of a rice field, as it had a " sugar bush " for making its maple sugar. The portion of a rice field was outlined by stakes, and a woman established her claim to it by going to the field about 10 days before the rice was ripe and tying portions of it in small sheaves. Basswood fiber is used without twisting for the tying of rice. One length is tied to another, making a large hard ball that unwinds from the middle. The ball is placed in a tray behind the woman as she sits in the canoe. For this work she wears a special waist (pl. 36, *a*), which, with the care of Chippewa women, is reenforced on the shoulder where the basswood fiber passes through a little birch-bark ring. This method of carrying the " twine " keeps it ready to her hand and free from becoming tangled. (Pl. 36, *b*.) She draws a little group of rice stalks toward her with the " rice hoop " (pl. 37) and winds the fiber around them, bending the tip of the sheaf or bundle down to the stalks. The process in detail is shown in Plate 38. The rice is left standing until ripe, when the sheaf is untied, the rice shaken out, and kept separate from the rest of the crop. (Pl. 39.) It has a slightly different flavor than other rice and the kernels are said to be heavier, requiring longer boiling.

When the time came for harvesting the rice a camp was established on the shore of a lake where rice was abundant. (Pl. 40, a.)

In this, as in the making of maple sugar, the unit was the family or group of immediate relatives, all of whom assisted in the process. Three rice camps were visited and photographed by the author during the harvest season. The equipment for " rice-making " comprised a canoe or boat with a propelling pole and two rice-beating sticks, one or more birch-bark rolls, the same size as for a wigwam cover, a kettle or tub for parching rice, and a peculiar paddle used for stirring the rice in the kettle; also a barrel sunk in the ground for the first pounding of the rice, and several pestles used for that purpose, several " winnowing trays " made of birch bark, and a small barrel sunk in the ground and having two bars beside it, this portion of the equipment being for "treading out " the final chaff from the rice. Receptacles for storing the rice were also provided, these in the older days being bags woven of cedar or basswood bark.

The manner of going through the rice field was by means of a canoe or boat pushed along by a pole forked at the end. (Pl. 40, b.) This was a heavy task and was usually performed by a man while a woman sat in the stern of the boat and harvested the rice.

In the early morning the canoes started for the rice field and did not return until about the middle of the afternoon, the time depending on the distance to be traveled. Sometimes the rice to be harvested was at the farther side of a lake, requiring considerable time to reach the spot. A canoeful of rice was considered a day's gathering. The harvesting of the " free rice " (that which had not been tied) was done by knocking the kernels off the stalk and allowing them to fall into the canoe. Two " rice-sticks " were used for this purpose. The stalks were bent down with one of them, and a sweeping but gentle stroke with the other stick liberated the kernels. (Pl. 40, c.) The rice at the right as well as the left of the boat was harvested in this manner, a woman using one hand as easily as the other in knocking off the kernels. It was considered a test of a good rice gatherer to free the ripe rice kernels without dislodging those which were unripe. Thus it was possible to go over the same part of a rice field several times at intervals of a few days, allowing time for more rice to ripen. It was not the intention, however, to harvest all the rice, a portion being allowed to fall into the water, or being sowed on the water as seed. The ideal weather for rice gathering was warm and still, as wind or rain dislodged the kernels.

GRANULATING TROUGH, STIRRING PADDLE, GRANULATING LADLES, AND MAKUK OF GRANULATED MAPLE SUGAR

a, CAKES OF MAPLE SUGAR AND MAKUK FILLED WITH SAME

b, STACKED DISHES AND EMPTY CONES, THE LATTER TO
BE FILLED WITH SUGAR

a, WAIST WORN WHEN TYING RICE (BACK VIEW)

b, WOMAN IN BOAT, TYING RICE

TIED RICE AND RICE HOOP

PROCESS OF TYING RICE

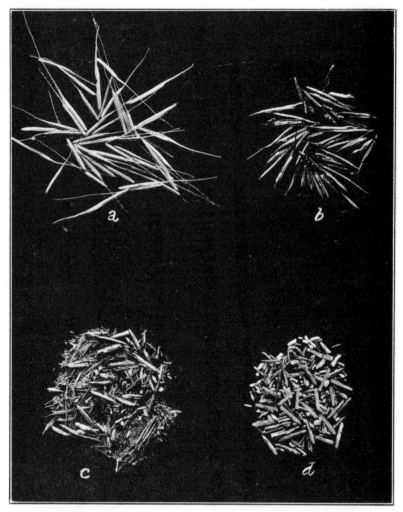

TIED RICE, SHOWING STAGES OF PREPARATION

a, RICE FIELD

b, POLING BOAT THROUGH RICE

c, HARVESTING RICE

a, RICE SPREAD TO DRY

b, PARCHING RICE

c, MORTAR FORMERLY USED IN POUNDING RICE

a, WINNOWING RICE

b, POUNDING RICE   *c*, TREADING RICE

a, PREPARED MEDICINAL SUBSTANCES TIED IN CLOTH

b, PACKET WRAPPED IN THIN BIRCH BARK

c, PACKETS OF LEAVES AND TWIGS READY FOR USE

d, PACKETS OF BARK READY FOR USE

In some camps the parching and threshing of the rice was done in the late afternoon and evening, and those who gathered the rice assisted in this portion of the work, but in a large camp this part of the process was carried on simultaneously with the gathering, those who remained in the camp parching and threshing while the rest were gathering.

When the canoes arrived the loads of rice were carried to the camp and spread on sheets of birch bark. (Pl. 41, a.) These had been placed where the sun would shine upon them, but not with such directness as to heat the rice, which was frequently stirred so it would be evenly dried. This was important, as at the season of rice gathering the nights are frequently cold with very hot sun in the middle of the day. About 24 hours was usually allowed for this preliminary drying, after which the rice was either parched in a kettle or dried over a slow fire. The first was the more common process, the rice being placed in a large kettle, or a metal tub, which was propped in a slanting position over the fire so that a woman seated beside it could stir the rice with a paddle. (Pl. 41, b.) The fire was carefully regulated and considerable skill was required to parch the rice without burning it. The quantity parched at a time was usually about a peck, and the required time about an hour. This parching loosened the husk and also imparted a flavor to the rice. The stirring paddle was slender and different in shape from that used with a canoe. The second is undoubtedly the oldest process, and produced what was known as " hard rice." This was greenish black in color, much darker than parched rice and requiring longer to cook. This rice could be kept indefinitely, and could be used for seed. In preparing " hard rice," a frame was made similar to that on which berries were dried. It was covered by a layer of hay on which the rice, either on stalks or in the husk, was spread to a depth of about 3 inches. A slow fire was kept burning beneath the frame. In this manner the rice was dried as vegetables or berries are dried.

The next process was the " pounding " of the rice. For this process the rice is frequently put into a barrel, but the best container for the purpose is a wooden mortar with sloping sides. (Pl. 41, c.) This was about the size of an ordinary barrel, and was made by the Indians and kept for this purpose. With this were used wooden pestles somewhat pointed at the end. In pounding the rice these moved up and down near the edge of the mortar, the pointed ends being adapted for this purpose. It is said these disturbed the kernels with the least breaking of the kernels. (Pl. 42, b.) Another form of a pestle was blunt at the end, nearly resembling a mallet. Both varieties were about 5½ feet long and in the correct pounding of the rice they were not heavily forced downward but allowed to drop of their own weight. This process was supposed to loosen the husk entirely without breaking the kernel. If the work was done carefully, the rice kernel was entirely freed from the husk.

The rice was then winnowed, either by tossing it in a tray or by pouring it slowly from a tray to birch bark put on the ground. The place chosen for this work was a place where the breeze would assist the process by blowing away the chaff. (Pl. 42, a.)

The final step in the process was the treading of the rice to dislodge the last fragments of the husk. For this purpose a small wooden receptacle, holding about a bushel, was partially sunk in the ground, and on either side of it was placed a stout pole, one end of which was fastened to a tree about 4 feet above the ground, the other end resting on the ground. The treading was done by a man wearing clean moccasins, and the poles were for him to rest his arms upon during the process. (Pl. 42, c.) The sole of the foot was peculiarly adapted to this work, as the husks having been removed, the kernels would have been easily broken by wooden instruments. In treading rice the action resembles that of dancing, the entire body being in action, with the weight not heavily placed on the feet. Leaning on the poles, straightening to full height, or moving his body with undulating, sinuous grace, the treader accomplished his part of the task. It is said that in old times a hole was dug in the ground and lined with deerskin, the rice being placed in this instead of a barrel. The chaff from this treading was usually kept and cooked similarly to the rice, having much the flavor of the rice, and being considered somewhat of a delicacy.

The stored rice was sewn in bags of various sizes, which were somewhat similar in use to the makuks in which maple sugar was stored. On top of the rice was laid straw, and the bags, like the makuks, were sewed across the top with basswood twine.

While rice making was an industry essential to the food supply, it had, like the sugar camp, a pleasant social phase, which was appreciated by old and young. Thus the writer in driving through the rice country late one afternoon came upon a camp of three or four tipis. The rice gatherers had returned from the fields, and the men were sitting on rush mats and smoking while the younger women stirred two parching kettles and an older woman tossed a winnowing tray. At a fire one woman was preparing the evening meal and at a distance another was seen chopping wood. Dogs and little children were running about, and the scene with its background of pines and shining lake was one of pleasure and activity.

An important part of the camp was its provisioning. Indians did not carry many supplies with them, and it is probable that in the old days many carried no provisions to a rice camp except maple sugar, which was used for seasoning all foods. At night the women set their fish nets and in the morning they drew them in, thus securing fish, some of which they dried. In one of the camps visited by the writer the top branches of a young Norway pine had been broken, and it was said that fish had been dried on these branches, the splinters forming a convenient frame. If ducks were available the hunters went out in the morning, and occasionally a deer was secured for the camp. The principal food, however, was the fresh rice, which was eaten either parched or boiled.

BEVERAGES

It is interesting to note that the Chippewa did not commonly drink water encountered in traveling but boiled it, making some of the following beverages from vegetable substances that were easily available. Fresh leaves were tied in a packet with a thin strip of basswood bark before being put in the water. (Pl. 43, *c*, at left.) Dried leaves could be used if fresh leaves were not available. The quantity was usually about a heaping handful to a quart of water. Beverages were usually sweetened with maple sugar and drunk while hot. The botanical name, common name, and portion of plant used are shown in the following list:

> *Ledum groenlandicum* Oeder. Labrador tea. Leaves.
> *Chiogenes hispidula* (L.) T. C. G. Creeping snowberry. Leaves.
> *Gaultheria procumbens* L. Wintergreen. Leaves.
> *Tsuga canadensis* (L.) Carr. Hemlock. Leaves.
> *Picea rubra* (Du Roi) Dietr. Spruce. Leaves.
> *Rubus strigosus* Michx. Red raspberry. Twigs.
> *Prunus virginiana* L. Chokecherry. Twigs.
> *Prunus serotina* Ehrh. Wild cherry. Twigs.

In preparing this last beverage the twigs of the chokecherry and wild cherry were tied in a little bundle by a strip of bark long enough to permit the lifting of the bundle and dropping it into hot water without burning the hand. The bundle of twigs for one infusion was about 4 inches long and each packet was perhaps 1 inch in diameter. (Pl. 43, *c*, at right.)

Maple sugar was dissolved in cold water and served as a drink in hot weather. This was offered to the writer and found to be pleasantly refreshing.

A Cass Lake informant said that his wife gathered all kinds of flowers and dried them in a wire basket, beginning with the first flowers in the spring and putting in a few of each variety as it appeared. He said that by the first of July she had more than twenty varieties. In the fall she pulverized them and stored them. A winter drink was made in the following manner: A quart of water was allowed to come to a boil and in it were placed a spoonful of the powdered flowers and a tiny bit of red pepper. The water was then removed from the stove and the mixture allowed to steep a short time.

SEASONINGS

Koellia virginiana (L.) MacM. Mountain mint.
    The flowers and buds were used to season either meat or broth.

Arctostaphylos uva-ursi (L.) Spreng. Bearberry.
    The red berries of this plant were cooked with meat as a seasoning for the broth. The leaves were smoked (see p. 337).

Asarum canadense L. Wild ginger.
    The root of this plant was regarded as an "appetizer," being put in any food as it was being cooked. It was also used for indigestion (see p. 342).

The silk of corn (called "corn hair") was dried before the fire and put in broth to season it. The corn silk was said to thicken the broth slightly as well as to impart a pleasing flavor.

Pumpkin blossoms were dried and used to thicken broth.

A Canadian Chippewa said that in old times his people had no salt and that more maple sugar was used as seasoning than the quantity of salt now used by white people. In the early days the Minnesota Chippewa had no salt and some of the older Indians have not yet acquired a taste for it. In a treaty known as the "Salt Treaty," [3] concluded at Leech Lake, August 21, 1847, with the Pillager Band of Chippewa, there was a stipulation that the Indians should receive 5 barrels of salt annually for five years.

A sirup was sometimes made from the sap of the woodbine and wild rice was boiled in it to give an agreeable flavor.

CEREALS

Zizania palustris L. Indian rice.

Wild rice was the principal cereal food of the Chippewa, being cooked alone and also with meat or game. The manner of procuring it and the first processes of its preparation have already been described. The following are among the ways in which rice was cooked:

(*a*) Boiled in water and eaten with or without maple sugar.

(*b*) Boiled with meat.

(*c*) Grease was put in a kettle and the rice parched in the grease, after which it was seasoned with maple sugar. Dried blueberries were often combined with this, and the rice and berries stored for use on journeys.

(*d*) Rice (not parched) was stored with dried blueberries during the winter and the two were cooked together in the spring.

---

[3] A compilation of all the treaties between the United States and the Indian tribes, now in force as laws. Washington, 1873, p. 212.

(*e*) Rice (parched when gathered) was prepared as follows: Boiling broth, either of meat or fish, was poured over parched rice, which was then covered and allowed to " steam " for a time until softened.

(*f*) The chaff from the treading of the rice was cooked similarly to the rice and was considered a delicacy.

Zea mays L. Corn.

Corn was cultivated in gardens by the Chippewa and prepared for use as follows:

(*a*) Fresh ears were roasted in the husks.

(*b*) The corn was cut before it was fully ripe. It was then shelled and dried by spreading it on sheets of birch bark. This was boiled and seasoned with maple sugar.

(*c*) The husks were turned back and the corn dried by suspending the ears by the husks from the ceiling.

(*d*) Corn was parched in a hot kettle, some of the kernels popping open and others drying. The corn was then put in a leather bag, laid on a flat stone, and pounded with another stone until it was like meal. This was made into " parched corn soup," to which deer tallow or deer meat, either fresh or dried, was added.

(*e*) Corn was made into " hominy." A lye was first made from hardwood ashes. The corn was boiled in this, rinsed, and boiled in clear water. Bones were sometimes boiled with it, and grease was added as seasoning. In addition to using the corn, the water in which it was boiled was considered very palatable.

VEGETABLES

Pumpkins and squashes were cultivated in gardens and either eaten fresh or cut in pieces or in strips for drying. These were laid on frames or were strung on long pieces of basswood cord and hung above the fire where the drying was slowly accomplished. They were stored in bags and sometimes kept for two years. Dried squash and pumpkin were boiled with game, or boiled alone and seasoned with maple sugar. The flowers of the latter were dried and used in broth for seasoning and also for thickening.

Other vegetable foods were obtained without cultivation, among them being the following:

Helianthus tuberosus L. (The original of the cultivated Jerusalem artichoke.)

The root of this plant was eaten raw like a radish.

Sagittaria latifolia Willd. Arrowhead.

This is commonly called the " wild potato," and grows in deep mud. At the end of the tubular roots are the " potatoes " which are gathered in the fall, strung, and hung overhead in the wigwam to dry. Later they are boiled for use.

Lycopus asper Greene. Bugleweed.

These were called " crow potatoes " and were dried and boiled.

Moss growing on white pine.

The moss was dried and stored. When used it was " put in water to freshen it up," and it was then boiled and put in fish or meat broth. It was said to be very nourishing.

Asclepias syriaca L. Common milkweed.

The flowers were cut up and stewed, being eaten like preserves. It is said that this plant was sometimes eaten before a feast, so that a man could consume more food.

Parthenocissus quinquefolia (L.) Greene. Woodbine.

The stalk was cut in short lengths and boiled, then peeled. Between the outer bark and the wood there was a sweetish substance which was eaten somewhat after the manner of eating corn from the cob. The water in which the woodbine had been boiled was then boiled down to a sirup. If sugar were lacking, wild rice was boiled in this sirup to season it.

Falcata comosa (L) Kuntze. Wild bean and hog peanut.

The root of this plant was boiled and eaten. It also had a medicinal value (see p. 289).

Scirpus validus Vahl. Bulrush.

On the root of these rushes there is a small bulb occurring at the turn of the root. If the rushes are pulled in midsummer this bulb has a sweetish taste and may be eaten raw.

Aster (species doubtful). Aster.

This plant grows near Lake Superior. The leaves are boiled with fish and eaten with the fish.

Populus tremuloides Michx. Aspen.

If the bark of the poplar is cut and turned back from the tree in the early summer there is found between the bark and the wood a sweetish sirup which can be put in birch bark and kept for a short time. This is especially liked by children and young people.

Quercus macrocarpa Muhl. Bur oak.

Sweet acorns (mĭtĭgo′ mĭnûm) were frequently gathered in the late fall and buried for use in the winter or spring, or they could be used as soon as they were gathered. They were cooked in three ways: (1) They were boiled, split open, and eaten like a vegetable; (2) roasted in the ashes; (3) boiled, mashed, and eaten with grease. They were said to be especially good with duck broth.

Tilia americana L. Basswood.

The sap next the bark was used similarly to the woodbine sirup.

A Canadian Chippewa said that he peeled the outside bark from the poplar and also the white birch, and scraped the inner bark, obtaining a little sap which they put in a small makuk. He said that it had a sweetish taste and " would keep quite a while."

FRUITS AND BERRIES

Crataegus (species doubtful). Thornapple.

These were prepared by squeezing them in the hands, after which they were made into little cakes without cooking, dried on birch-bark and stored to be cooked in winter.

Prunus virginiana L. Chokecherry.

These were pounded, stones and all, between two stones, and dried similarly to the thornapples.

Vitis cordifolia Michx. Grape.

Eaten raw.

Cornus canadensis L. Bunchberry.

Berries eaten raw.

Fragaria virginiana Duchesne. Strawberry.

Berries eaten raw.

All the following berries were eaten raw as well as dried for winter use.

Prunus serotina Ehrh. Wild cherry.
Ribes triste Pall. Red currant.
Ribes species. Wild currant.
Prunus americana Marsh. Chokecherry.
Rubus frondosus Bigel (?). Blackberry.
Rubus strigosus Michx. Red raspberry.

The berries were cooked without sugar, spread on birch bark in little cakes and dried, the cakes then stored in a birch-bark makuk for winter use.

Amelanchier canadensis (L.) Medic. Shadbush.

These are called " Juneberries " by the Chippewa and are found abundantly in their country. They are considered the simplest form of refreshment. " Take some Juneberries with you," is a common saying among the Chippewa. A certain song contains the words " Juneberries I would take to eat on my journey if I were a son-in-law." [4]

Oxycoccus macrocarpus (Ait.) Pers. Cranberry. Cooked, probably with sugar.
Vaccinium angustifolium Ait. Blueberry.

---

[4] Bull. 53, Bur. Amer. Ethn., song No. 169.

A Canadian Chippewa said that his people combined dried blue-berries with moose fat and deer tallow.

All dried berries were boiled when used, and either seasoned with maple sugar or combined with other foods.

PLANTS AS MEDICINE

TREATMENT BY MEANS OF PLANTS

It must be conceded that the use of plants by the Indians was based upon experiment and study. The Indians say that they " received this knowledge in dreams," but the response of the physical organism was the test of a plant as a remedy. As the physical organism is the same in both races it should not be a matter of surprise that some of the remedies used by the Indians are found in the pharmacopœia of the white race. An observer of the Cree Indians writes: "Although the list of materia medica is a small one there is remarkable judgment shown in the choice of remedies. Thus . . . the bark of the juniper and Canada balsam tree are doubtless as good an application to wounds as a people unversed in antiseptic application and ignorant of the existence of bacteria could devise. The use of *Lobelia* as an emetic and of *Iris versicolor* as a cholagogue and purgative approaches closely to the practice of more civilized nations.[5]

Health and long life represented the highest good to the mind of the Chippewa, and he who had knowledge conducive to that end was most highly esteemed among them. He who treated the sick, by whatever means, claimed that his knowledge came from *manido* (spirits), and those who saw a sick man restored to health by that knowledge readily accepted its origin as supernatural.

Two methods of treating the sick were in use among the Chippewa.[6] Both methods depended upon what was termed " supernatural aid," but material remedies were used in one and not in the other. The " doctors " who used material remedies were usually members of the Midewiwin, and their remedies were among the secrets of that organization. He who treated the sick without material means was called a *djasakid* (commonly translated " juggler ")[7] His procedure included the apparent swallowing and regurgitating of short tubular bones. (Pl. 46, *g*.)

It is a teaching of the Midewiwin that every tree, bush, and plant has a use. A country of such bountiful vegetation as that of the Chippewa presents a great amount of this material. Although the

---

[5] Holmes, E. M. (F. L. S.), " Medicinal plants used by the Cree Indians, Hudson's Bay Territory," The Pharmaceutical Journal and Transactions, 3d ser. vol. 15, pp. 303–304. London, 1884–85. See also Bur. Amer. Ethn. Bull. 61, p. 271.

[6] Cf. Bur. Amer. Ethn. Bull. 45, pp. 92–125; Bull. 61, pp. 244–278; Bull. 75, pp. 127–141.

[7] See Bur. Amer. Ethn. Bull. 45, pp. 119–125.

Midewiwin was a respository of knowledge of herbs it did not have a pharmacopœia accessible to every member. The remedies are individual, not general, and an individual when questioned invariably replies, " I can tell you about my own medicines. I do not know about other peoples' medicines nor their uses of the same plants." Thus it is frequently found that different people have different names and uses for the same plant. Members of the Midewiwin were not taught many remedies at once, except at the time of their initiation. Their instruction at that time comprised what might be termed a " ground work in the practice of medicine," with the identification and use of a number of plants. The same sort of instruction accompanied their advancement from one degree to another, and was made more extensive as they went into the higher degrees. Aside from these times of special instruction a man learned one or two remedies at a time as he felt inclined to go to the old men and buy the knowledge. Among the Chippewa, as among other tribes studied by the writer, it is not common for one man to treat a large number of diseases. A Sioux said:

" In the old days the Indians had few diseases, and so there was not a demand for a large variety of medicines. A medicine man usually treated one special disease and treated it successfully. He did this in accordance with his dream. A medicine man would not try to dream of all herbs and treat all diseases, for then he could not expect to succeed in all nor to fulfill properly the dream of any one herb or animal. He would depend on too many and fail in all. That is one reason why our medicine men lost their power when so many diseases came among us with the advent of the white man." [7a]

While many remarkable cures were said to have been wrought by the Mide remedies, it was said that if no improvement were seen in a reasonable time the treatment was usually discontinued, it being said that the medicine evidently would not " take hold " in that particular case. From this it seems possible that they recognized a self-limited, and also an incurable disease, and in such cases did not wish to raise the hopes of the patient.

The men and women who at the present time (1918) treat the sick by Mide remedies are well poised and keen eyed, with a manner which indicates confidence in themselves, and which would inspire confidence in the sick persons to whom they minister.

As already indicated, the medicinal use of herbs has been handed down for many generations in the Midewiwin. It is said that members of the Midewiwin " follow the bear path " in proceeding from a lower to a higher degree in the society and that some of the best Mide remedies were received from the bear. Thus one of the

---

[7a] Bull. 61, Bur. Amer. Ethn., pp. 244–245.

strongest medicines in the accompanying series (*Apocynum sp.*) is known as a "bear medicine." The roots of the "bear medicine" were cut in pieces about 2 inches long and strung on a cord when stored for use. Such a string of roots bore some resemblance to a necklace of bear claws. In this connection we note that the bear was highly esteemed by the Sioux medicine men, two of whom made the following statements:

Two Shields said:

"The bear is the only animal which is dreamed of as offering to give herbs for the healing of man. The bear is not afraid of either animals or men and it is considered ill-tempered, and yet it is the only animal which has shown us this kindness; therefore the medicines received from the bear are supposed to be especially effective."

In somewhat similar manner Siyaka said:

"The bear is quick-tempered and is fierce in many ways, and yet he pays attention to herbs which no other animal notices at all. The bear digs these for his own use. The bear is the only animal which eats roots from the earth and is also especially fond of acorns, June berries, and cherries. These three are frequently compounded with other herbs in making medicine, and if a person is fond of cherries we say he is like a bear. We consider the bear as chief of all animals in regard to herb medicine, and therefore it is understood that if a man dreams of a bear he will be expert in the use of herbs for curing illness. The bear is regarded as an animal well acquainted with herbs because no other animal has such good claws for digging roots." [8]

The material in the following chapter was obtained from three classes of informants: (1) Those who are active adherents of the Mide but were willing to tell of its remedies in order that a record of them might be preserved for posterity; (2) those who have renounced the Mide but continue to use its remedies either personally or in treating sick persons; and (3) those who have never been members of the Mide but have received a knowledge of its remedies from relatives who were members of the society. Among the principal informants on this subject at White Earth were Mrs. Brunett, Mrs. Gagewin, and Mrs. Louisa Martin. (Pl. 44.)

In the old days a person would not transmit any facts concerning medicines to even a member of his own family without compensation, one reason for this restriction seeming to be a fear that the information would not be treated with proper respect. So great was the secrecy surrounding these remedies that names were seldom given to plants, the person imparting the information showing the fresh plant. It was difficult, if not impossible, to recognize a root after it had been dried and rubbed into shreds, but medicine men frequently

---

[8] Bull. 61, Bur. Amer. Ethn., p. 195.

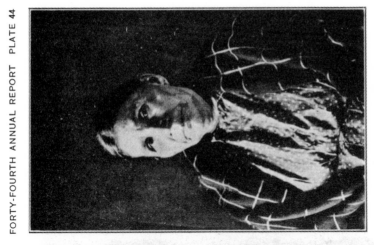

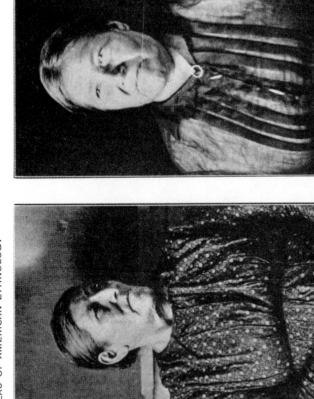

a, MRS. BRUNETT

b, MRS. GAGEWIN

c, MRS. LOUISA MARTIN

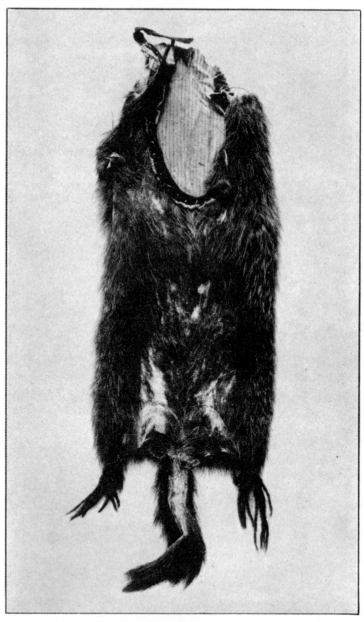

BAG IN WHICH MEDICINES HAVE BEEN KEPT

combined an aromatic herb with their medicines as a precaution against their identification. The fact that persons were willing to impart their knowledge of these ancient remedies for publication indicates that the attitude of the Chippewa toward their old customs is passing away.

There seems to have been something symbolic in the appearance of certain medicinal roots. The writer showed a certain root to a medicine woman and asked her if she knew what it was. She replied that its use was familiar to her, but that she would have known it was a medicinal root if she had never seen it before. On being questioned further she said it was evidently an old root which had sent up a new stalk each year and had long roots extending downward. The stalk and the small roots were gone, but the life remained in the root itself, and this would be the part used for medicine. A class of plants highly valued as medicines are those having a divided tap root supposed to resemble the legs of a man. An example of this is spikenard. The medicine woman already quoted brought the writer a plant which she said she had hesitated a long time before showing. Her affection and admiration for the plant itself were evident as she caressed its straight stalk, delicate leaves, and fine white roots, reluctant at the last to part with it.

In some instances the fertile and sterile plants were considered separately. It will be noted that a remedy for dysentery stipulates that the flowering plant of *Artemisia dracunculoides* (mugwort) be used, and that in a decoction for strengthening the hair it is stated that a sterile plant of the same be used. The writer was informed of a remedy in which both sorts of "rattlesnake root" were used, but it was impossible at the time to secure specimens for identification.

Vegetable remedies were usually gathered in the late summer or early fall, when the plants are fully developed. At that season it was customary for the Chippewa to take journeys or to send to other localities to obtain plants which grew in various soils.

An unfailing custom of the Mide in gathering plants for medicinal use is to dig a little hole in the ground beside the plant and put tobacco in the hole, speaking meanwhile to the plant. Gagewin, who is a member of the Mide, said that when he dug a plant he spoke somewhat thus: "You were allowed to grow here for the benefit of mankind, and I give you this tobacco to remind you of this, so that you will do the best you can for me." This, of course, is only representative of part of such a speech. On one occasion the writer saw the tobacco put beside a tree whose bark was to be used. The medicine man was a member of the Otter Tail Band of Chippewa. He said this was commanded by the *manido*, who gave all knowledge of plants to the Chippewa. He seemed to require no other authority or reason.

The part of the plant most commonly used was the root. In a majority of instances the whole root was used, but in some plants the healing power was supposed to be strongest in a certain portion of the root. Thus in dogbane the part preferred was the elbow of the root, the plant having a root which descends straight downward for 15 to 18 inches and then turns sharply to one side. In other instances the part used was the fine white roots depending from the larger root.

If stalks, leaves, or flowers were to be used as remedies they were dried by hanging them with the top downward and kept as clean as possible. After being dried, each variety was tied or wrapped separately for storage. Bark was gathered when the sap was in the tree but roots intended for future medicinal use were gathered before the sap started in the spring or after it had gone down in the fall. An informant at Cass Lake said that roots were not washed, the dirt being carefully shaken from them, but informants at White Earth said the roots were washed. After drying, they were tied in packets and stored in bags unless it was desired to have some special root ready for immediate use. Such a root was pulverized and stored in that form. Certain roots, when used, were broken in short pieces and boiled or steeped, but a majority were prepared for use either by pounding until they were in shreds or by pulverizing them in the hands, the latter being always done if the roots were small. The most common method of pulverizing roots was to place them in the palm of the left hand and then to rub them either with the thick portion of the right hand below the thumb or with the fingers of the right hand. Some Chippewa used a small round stone for this purpose, the stone having a shallow depression in which the medicine was mixed by rubbing with the thumb. If several sorts of roots were to be used in combination they were usually "pounded together" before they were stored, in order that they might be fully blended. Mrs. English said that she was once in a lodge where the medicine men were pounding their medicines on a stone and putting them in little bags. A stuffed owl was placed beside them. After leaving the lodge she asked about the owl and the reply was, "They always have to have someone watch to see that they do it right." [9]

The detailed instructions given concerning medicines is shown by the following example. An informant at Red Lake said that her great-grandmother taught her the use of herbs. This informant described one remedy for a certain injury and said that if it were not effective she would use another plant which was about a foot high and had no flowers. (A specimen was obtained but it was not perfect

---

[9] At a remote point north of Vermilion Lake, Minnesota, the writer visited the house of a medicine man and saw two owls (or owlskins) swinging from the branches of trees, suspended by a cord around their necks and drying. Several small animals were drying in other trees.

enough for identification.) She said, "The plant has a very long root and the leaves come up from joints of the root, not from the knuckle of the root which projects above the ground and is bare. I look for the knuckle or knob of the root and then look about 3 or 4 inches away for the leaves. The plant grows in soft ground, like that near a lake."

Medicinal barks were so generally available that they were usually gathered when they were needed. The barks of chokecherry and wild cherry, in quantity for one decoction, are shown in Plate 43, *d*, as they would be prepared for a patient.

As already stated, the roots and herbs were usually stored in bags. Some men used the square bags woven of yarn; others preferred bags woven of the inner bark of cedar. One old medicine man had a bag peculiarly adapted for holding medicinal roots. It was made of leather and was smaller at the top than at the bottom to preclude the possibility of dampness. The prepared pulverized roots could be kept in either birch bark or leather, the latter being preferred. A bag used for this purpose is shown in Plate 45. A packet of medicine tied in cloth ready to be delivered to a sick person is shown in Plate 43, *a*. This contains four vegetable substances pounded together and was said to be a sufficient quantity to make four liquid preparations of the remedy. This has no distinguishing mark, the ingredients being known only to the medicine man who prescribed the remedy. A medicine man, however, has various means of marking his herbs. One man identifies his prepared herbs by the knot in the string with which the packet is tied, the identification and use of the herbs being known only to himself.[9a]

The storing of roots in bags has already been noted and refers to a man's supply of roots and herbs for an entire season. Apart from this stored supply a member of the Mide usually carried a large number of medicines in his Mide bag. Sometimes he carried a small quantity of some particularly strong medicine in a buckskin bag, which was placed in the skull of the animal which formed his Mide bag. Poisons were not infrequently carried by the Mide, and they were instructed in their use. An instance was related of an aged man, a member of the Mide, who came to a lodge one winter night tired and cold. He said, "Never mind, I have some medicine which will soon warm me." He then took a packet from the skull of his Mide bag, put a little of the contents in water and drank it. A few moments later he said, "I have taken the wrong medicine; I shall die." And in a few hours he was dead.

In addition to the vegetable substances believed to have an effect when administered internally or externally there were herbs and roots believed to act by their presence independent of actual contact.

[9a] See Bull. 86, Bur. Amer. Ethn., Pl. 78, *b*.

These comprised substances which attracted (as love charms and the
hunting or fishing charms); also those which repelled (as those
which, carried on the person, were said to keep reptiles away); and
those which acted as an antidote to "bad medicine" carried by
another person. Among the latter is a certain plant the smoke of
which was supposed to counteract the effect of poison placed where
a person would step on it; also a combination of plants rubbed on
the limbs of a dancer to counteract the effect of medicine worn by
others with the intention of "tiring him out." Certain roots were
also chewed for the same purpose. In some instances it was said
that plants acted in both these ways, being worn as a protection, and
taken internally as a healing agency. Such were some of the medicines carried by warriors. Certain remedies were used exclusively
for horses, and some were used for both men and horses.

In addition to the special knowledge of plants held by the Mide,
there was a general knowledge of the simpler remedies, each household having a supply of such herbs for common ailments. If these
failed and the illness appeared to be serious, they sent for the man
whom they believed to have the proper remedy.

The names of plants are of several sorts. Thus we note
(1) names which indicate the place where the plant grows, as
" prairie sturgeon plant "; (2) names which describe the appearance
of the plant, as " squirrel tail " or " plump root "; (3) names which
describe their taste, as " bitter root "; and (4) names indicating the
part of the plant to be used, as " crow leaf." The names of the uses
of a plant, or a designation of the remedy is sometimes given as the
name of the plant itself, as (1) names indicating the use, as " head
medicine "; (2) names indicating the origin of the remedy, as "Winabojo remedy "; and (3) names denoting the power of the remedy,
as " chief medicine," which is applied to several highly esteemed
plants. With such a system of nomenclature it is evident that plants
of different species will have the same name and that in many instances a plant may be called by several different names. Thus the
purple mint was given three names by as many people.

The manner of preparing roots has already been described.
Stalks, leaves, and flowers were usually pulverized in a similar manner, though in one remedy it was prescribed that eight stems be used
in 1 quart of water. If bark were to be used the outer skin was
removed and the " inner bark " scraped or removed in long thin
strips which were boiled, either with or without pulverizing. An
informant said that the only regulation concerning the scraping
was that the root of alder must be scraped toward the plant.

Vegetable substances were further prepared for use by combining
them with water. Some were boiled a few moments, others were
allowed to come to a boil, then removed from the fire, and others

were scalded or steeped. Some roots were boiled in a thin sirup made of maple sugar, to give a pleasant flavor. Poultices and compresses were made by moistening the pounded fresh or dry roots or herbs. The strength of a decoction varied with the nature of the root and the age of the patient. A common proportion was a " hand-hollow-ful " of pulverized root to about a quart of water, but some roots were exceedingly strong and required special direction. Thus one root (calamus), although only about one-eighth of an inch in diameter, was so strong that the quantity used was measured by the length of the patient's index finger, whether an infant or an adult.

It was the author's intention to collect herbs which have medicinal use when administered singly. This presented some difficulties, as the Chippewa use combinations of herbs, sometimes as many as 20 vegetable substances being combined in one remedy. One medicine woman who practices medicine widely for money at the present time called special attention to the value of herbs in combinations. She appeared to attach more importance to combinations than to specifics, except in instances of simple definite value. While the tabulated lists (pp. 336–367) contain some combinations it will be noted that almost without exception each herb is considered efficacious if used alone. In some instances the combination of the herbs shows an interesting and intelligent purpose.

The quantity for a decoction and the size of a dose were difficult to determine with any degree of accuracy. One medicine woman who was particularly careful in her statements brought the pail in which she usually prepared her remedies, and it was found to hold about a pint. It appeared that she prepared smaller quantities than other persons, as a majority said they prepared their medicines in a lard pail, filling it to within $1\frac{1}{2}$ or 2 inches of the top. In the tabulated list of remedies the quantity of water is given as a quart, except in remedies prepared by the above-mentioned woman, for whose preparations a smaller amount is designated. Decoctions were usually boiled five or ten minutes. In only two instances (see pp. 339, 365) was there anything partaking of a ceremonial character in the preparing of liquid medicines, it being said that " the talking was all done when the roots were dug." In one of these instances there was something resembling a divination, the doctor watching the manner in which the powdered roots lay in the water and deciding thereby whether the medicine would be effective. The person who described this remedy was well versed in the ways of the Mide and said she had never heard of this being done in the preparation of any other remedy.

Liquid medicine was not measured when taken. A "large swallow " constituted an average dose, but a cupful was occasionally taken. The interval between the doses varied, as might be expected among a people who in old times were without timepieces. If the patient were in great suffering he was told to take the medicine, "at short intervals," understood to be about half an hour. In what was probably a majority of cases the patient took the medicine "at frequent intervals," or whenever he felt inclined. Sometimes he was instructed to "drink it freely," or drink some after an attack of coughing. These directions were given by the person who prepared the medicine, and who gave various other instructions, such as rest after taking the medicine, or abstinence from food. In a majority of cases it was expected that improvement, though perhaps slight, would be evident after three or four doses had been taken.

Remedies were administered externally in the following manner:

(1) Fresh roots or leaves were macerated and applied.

(2) Dried roots or leaves were pulverized, prepared in the form of a decoction, and applied.

(3) Dried roots or leaves were pulverized, moistened, and applied like a poultice.

(4) Dried roots or leaves were pulverized and strewn on hot stones, the treatment being by the fumes.

(5) A decoction was sprinkled on hot stones, the treatment being by steam.

(6) Herbs were boiled with grease for a salve.

(7) Dried and powdered roots were mixed with grease and used as an emollient.

Remedies were administered internally in the following manner:

(1) Dried powdered roots or leaves were either boiled or steeped in water.

(2) Dried powdered roots were used as snuff, or prepared with lukewarm water.

(3) Fresh roots or herbs were chewed.

(4) Slight incisions were made with a bit of sharp glass or flint, and dried, powdered roots placed over the incisions.

(5) Remedies were "pricked into the skin" with a set of needles used for that purpose.

(6) Pulverized roots were mixed with "red willow" or tobacco and smoked in a pipe.

(7) A decoction of herbs was administered as an enema.

SUBSTANCES OTHER THAN VEGETABLE USED AS REMEDIES

(1) Deer tallow and bear grease were used as emollients, either alone or mixed with vegetable substances.

(2) Bear's gall, dried, was used in connection with cedar charcoal, being "pricked into the skin" with needles. (See p. 333.)

(3) Bumblebees, dried, were used with the root of alder. (See p. 359.)

(4) Red pipestone was used as a remedy for scrofulous neck and was said to cause the swelling to go down gradually without breaking into an open sore. The directions were: " Grate red pipestone to a powder, take a teaspoonful dry, then drink water. Take it once a day, two or three times a week."

(5) Clamshell was used as a remedy for ulcer, the directions being as follows: " Burn a clamshell, powder it finely in the hand, mix it with bear's grease or any soft grease, using only enough to hold it together. The mixing is usually done in a clamshell. Apply to the sore or ulcer."

MEDICAL APPLIANCES

(1) The lodge in which a sweat bath was taken has been described in connection with customs of the Midewiwin.[9b] The same procedure was used if a person were suffering from a very bad cold and was feverish. No medicine was put in the water which was sprinkled on the stones. After the bath the person was thoroughly rubbed, warmly wrapped, and put to bed. This bath was taken by hunters when they returned weary, or by anyone who wished to be refreshed; also by those inclined to rheumatism.

(2) Another method of steaming was used chiefly for rheumatic limbs, and with the water they put any sort of medicine which was supposed to be good for that ailment. In giving this treatment a hole was dug in the ground the size of the kettle containing the hot decoction. They put the kettle into this hole and the person sat beside it, covering his limbs closely with a blanket. A medicine frequently used in this connection was identified as willow (species doubtful). The prepared root was put in hot water and allowed to boil a short time. It was usually cooled before using.

(3) Dry herbs were also placed on heated stones and the fumes were inhaled, this treatment being used chiefly for headache. The stones were somewhat smaller than those used in the sweat lodge, being "about the size of a small bowl." The patient covered his head and shoulders with a blanket, inclosing the stones and inhaling the fumes. A mixture of many varieties of flowers was said to be an agreeable preparation for this use.

(4) A simple appliance was a strip of slippery elm bark which was often used in place of an emetic, the soft inner bark being used and inserted in the throat.

(5) Apparatus for enema. It is said that the early Chippewa understood the administering of both nourishment and medicine by means of enema. The apparatus for this consisted of a syringe, a small birch-bark tray on which the syringe was laid, and two meas-

---

[9b] See Bull. 86, Bur. Amer. Ethn., p. 94.

ures for the medicine, a larger one for adults and a smaller one for children. The syringe was composed of the bladder of the deer. The proper amount of medicine was put into this bladder, then a short piece of clean hollow rush was tied in the opening by means of a strip of wet slippery elm, the rush projecting about an inch. This was used only once and then burned. The principal medicines administered in this manner were (a) the inner bark of the common white birch. This was scraped and about a hand-hollow steeped in water; (b) the wood of a tree identified as *Fraxinus*. A hand-hollow of this was steeped in water. A small spatula for powdered herbs and a measure for liquid medicine are shown in Plate 46, a and h.

SURGICAL TREATMENT AND APPLIANCES

(1) The letting of blood was a remedial measure frequently used among the Chippewa and was resorted to for numerous causes. The principal instrument used in this treatment was a small pointed blade set in a handle about 3 or 4 inches long. (Pl. 46.) By means of this instrument blood was taken from the forearm or from the ankle. In using this instrument the part to be cut was firmly stroked downward, forcing the blood to the extremity; a bandage was then applied above the point at which the incision was to be made. In making the incision the instrument was held close to the flesh and lightly snapped with the thumb and finger of the right hand, thus inflicting a slight incision of the vein. If too much force were applied, the result might be fatal; thus an instance was related in which the vein was entirely severed and the man died. It is said that about "half a basin" of blood was usually taken. A medicine to check the bleeding was then applied and the upper bandage removed. The root commonly used for this purpose was identified as *Drymocallis arguta* (Pursh.) Rydb. The prepared root was either used dry or was moistened with warm water, placed on soft duck down, and laid over the incision. It was said by three informants that this treatment was used especially for persons who had met with an accident, as a fall or an injury to the back, and that the medicine "prevented the blood from settling in one place." This treatment was also used for "persons who seemed to have too much blood."

(2) A surgical treatment in common use consisted in cutting small gashes from which a small amount of blood was removed. These gashes were formerly made with a piece of sharp flint, but in later times a piece of thick glass is carefully broken so as to leave a sharp splinter, which is used for this purpose. This is kept in a leather shield or covering (pl. 46, c, d), and is used as a lancet according to the general use of that instrument. These cuts might be made in various parts of the body. The writer saw a woman whose elbow had

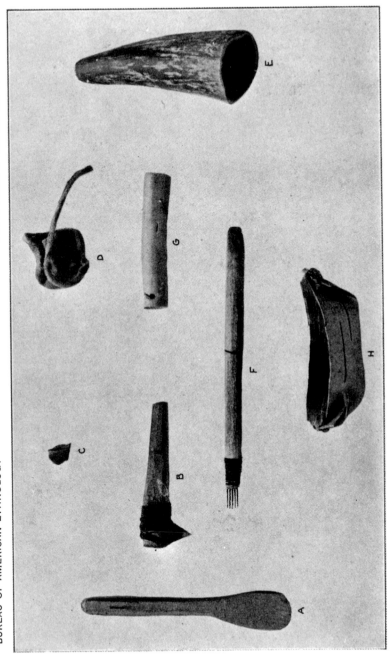

SURGICAL APPLIANCES

A, Small spatula for powdered herbs; *B*, Lance; *C, D*, Flint used as lance and its leather case; *E*, Horn used in drawing blood to the skin; *F*, Instrument for applying medicine beneath the skin; *G*, Bone apparently swallowed by djasakid; *H*, Birch-bark measure for liquid medicine

been cut with 15 or 20 gashes about a quarter of an inch long. This treatment was given for a sprain, her elbow having swollen to twice its natural size. The most common use of this treatment was for headache, as described below, but it was used for any inflammation. A remedy for the bite of a snake was administered in this manner, the plant being identified as *Plantago major* L.

(3) In connection with the incisions above described there was a small horn (pl. 46, *e*) if the treatment was for headache. In this treatment about six very short, deep incisions were made on the temples with the flint or glass, after which the doctor placed the larger end of the horn over the incisions and applied his mouth to the smaller end, sucking until the blood came to the surface. He then quickly removed his lips from the horn, placed his finger over the small end of the horn and lowered it so that the blood would run into it. When enough had been removed he wiped the skin and applied a healing medicine, as noted above, or some remedy for headache, or he might place a moist compress or " grease " over the cuts. This cutting of the temples was also used for inflammation of the eyes.

(4) An instrument for applying medicine beneath the skin consisted of several needles fastened at the end of a wooden handle (pl. 46, *f*). This was used in treating " dizzy headache," neuralgia, or rheumatism in any part of the body. In giving the treatment the medicine was " worked in " with the needles. If only a small part were to be " gone over " it was customary to hold a knife in the left hand and to use the blade as a guide for the needles. These were " worked up and down " close to the blade, " which kept the medicine from spreading." The remedy used most often in this manner was made as follows: Hazel stalks or cedar wood was burned to a charcoal and a small quantity of the charcoal (or ash) was mixed with an equal quantity of the dried gall of a bear. It was mixed well and placed in a birch-bark dish. When used it was moistened a little with water and stirred, after which a little was taken on the blade at the end of the wooden instrument and laid on the affected part. It was then " worked in " with the needles. The dark spots seen on the temples of many Indians are left by the charcoal in this medicine. A remedy for rheumatism was applied in a similar manner. The plant was identified as *Trillium grandiflorum* (Michx.) Salisb., and it was used in the form of a decoction.

(5) The use of a knife in amputation was mentioned by Maĭŋ'gans, whose limbs were amputated below the knee, the only instrument used being a common knife. When he was a boy his feet and limbs were badly frozen and in a hopeless condition. The pain was so intense that he begged a man to amputate them in this manner, and

he did so. This was followed by a dressing of pounded bark (*Prunus serotina* Ehrh.) applied dry and renewed as often as it became damp—usually twice a day. Nothing else was used and the healing was perfect.

(6) Another use of the knife in surgery was described by Wezawaŋge, who said he had treated a case in which this became necessary. It was a gangrenous wound, and he used the knife, not to remove, but to "loosen" the affected flesh, which was taken out by the medicine he applied. He said that in a case of this sort everything must be very clean, care being taken especially that the knife or remedies did not come in contact with rust. In this treatment he said that he used a medicine which had been handed down by the Mide and was particularly valued. It consisted of the inner bark of the white pine, the wild plum, and the wild cherry, it being necessary to take the first two from young trees. The writer saw him cut a young pine tree for this purpose and place tobacco in the ground close to the root before doing so. In preparing the medicine he said that the stalk of the pine was cut in short sections and boiled with the green inner bark of the other two trees until all the bark was soft. The water should be renewed when necessary, and the last water saved for later use. The bark was then removed from the pine stems and all the bark mashed with a heavy hammer until it was a pulp. It was then dried, and when needed it was moistened with the water which had been kept for that purpose. He said this medicine was usually prepared when needed, as the materials were so readily at hand. This wet pulp was applied to any wound or to a fresh cut and was a healing remedy, but was especially used for neglected wounds which had become gangrenous.

(7) Splints were placed on fractured limbs. The splints were best when made of very thick birch bark similar to that used for canoes. The birch bark was heated and bent to the proper shape, after which it was as rigid as plaster of Paris. Splints were also made of thin cedar. Tying the splint with basswood twine added greatly to its rigidity.

The treatment of a fractured arm was described as follows: "Wash the arm with warm water and apply grease. Then apply a warm poultice, cover with a cloth and bind with a thin cedar splint." The roots used for the poultice were *Asarum canadense* L. (wild ginger) and *Aralia racemosa* L. (spikenard).

These two were dried and mashed together in equal parts. The directions added "when poultice becomes dry it should be renewed, or, if the arm is very tender, the poultice may be moistened with warm water without removing it."

(8) Old women whose limbs or knees were weak often made supports by taking wide strips of fresh basswood bark and binding it

around their limbs in a kind of splint. When dried it was very hard and supported their limbs so that they could travel.

(9) The splinters from a tree struck by lightning were always carried by medicine men and used as lances, especially for lancing the gums. If a man were suffering from toothache they cut the gum with these splinters " so that the blood ran."

DENTAL SURGERY

If a tooth were hollow the Chippewa sometimes heated an awl or other metal instrument almost red hot and put it into the hollow of the tooth.

If it were considered necessary to pull a tooth they struck it forcibly to loosen it.

If a tooth were partly loosened they tied a sinew around the tooth, close to the root, attached it to something solid and pulled the tooth by jerking backward.

CLASSIFICATION OF DISEASES AND INJURIES [10]

1. Nervous system:
    Convulsions.
    Headache.
    " Craziness."
2. Circulatory system:
    Heart.
    In the blood.
3. Respiratory system:
    Cold.
    Cough.
    Lung trouble.
    Hemorrhage from lungs.
4. Digestive system:
    Sore mouth.
    Toothache.
    Sore throat.
    Indigestion.
    Pain.
    Colic.
    Cramps.
    Dysentery.
    Physic (use of).
    Emetics (use of).
    Worms.
    Cholera infantum.
5. Urinary system:
    Kidney trouble.
    Stoppage of urine.
    Gravel.
6. Skin:
    Inflammation.
    Boils.
    Sores.
    Eruptions.
    Warts.
    Hair.
7. Wounds:
    Incised.
    Internal.
    Bites of poisonous reptiles.
8. Bruises.
9. Burns.
10. Ulcers.
11. Fevers.
12. Scrofula.
13. Hemorrhages.
14. Diseases of women.
15. Diseases of the eye.
16. Diseases of the ear.
17. Diseases of the joints, including rheumatism and sprains.
18. Baths.
19. Tonics and stimulants.
20. Enemas.
21. General remedies.
22. Diseases of the horse.

[10] In determining this basis of classification the author received the valued assistance of Dr. D. S. Lamb, who at the time was pathologist at the Army Medical Museum, Washington, D. C.

System or part affected	Symptoms	Botanical name	Part of plant used
Nervous system........	Convulsions.........	Lathyrus venosus Muhl. (Wild pea.)	Root [1]...........
Do..............	....do..............	Lathyrus venosus Muhl..........	....do...........
		Apocynum androsaemifolium L.† (Dogbane.)	....do...........
Do..............	....do..............	Hepatica americana Ker. (Hepatica.)	....do...........
Do..............	....do..............	Solidago juncea Ait. (Goldenrod)..	....do...........
Do..............	....do..............	Polygala senega L. (Seneca snakeroot.)	....do...........
		Artemisia frigida Willd. (Prairie sage.)	....do...........
		Astragalus crassicarpus Nutt. (Ground plum.)	....do...........
		Rosa arkansana Porter, (Wild rose).	....do...........
Do..............	Headache..........	Apocynum androsaemifolium L.† (Dogbane.)	....do.[3]...........
Do..............	....do..............	Achillea millefolium L.† (Yarrow.)	Leaves...........
Do..............	....do..............	Arctostaphylos uva-ursi (L.) Spreng.† (Bearberry.)	....do...........
Do..............	....do..............	Polygonatum commutatum. (R. & S.) Dietr. (Solomonseal.)	Root...........
Do..............	....do..............	Pulsatilla hirsutissima (Pursh) Britton.† (Pasque flower.)	Leaves...........

[1] Unless otherwise stated, it is understood that roots, leaves, flowers, and stalks are dried and rubbed into powder or shreds before using. (See p. 326.)

[3] A decoction was boiled. Concerning the manner of making decoctions and the dosage see p. 329. Certain remedies were steeped instead of boiled, a distinction being made between the two modes of preparation.

How prepared	How administered	Remarks and references
Decoction ³_____	Internally_____	
Decoction; the first-named root was so strong that the amount used was measured from the last joint to the tip of the little finger. The amount of the second was about 1 foot of the root.	If the convulsions were so severe that only a little of the decoction could be forced into the patient's mouth the decoction was sprinkled on the chest and applied to the palms of the hands and soles of the feet.	There were said to be 8 varieties of the first plant which were equally good. See hemorrhages and tonics.
Decoction; 1 root to 1 quart of water.	Internally_____	Used chiefly for children.
_____do_____	_____do_____	
Decoction_____	_____do_____	See Hemorrhages; tonics and charms (for the latter use the first-named plant is used alone).
(1) Dried and pulverized_____	4 pieces of dried root about the size of a pea were pulverized and the dry powder snuffed up the nostrils.	This herb was used not simply for a pain in the head but for a serious affection of the nerves of which the headache was the symptom. It was given for "excessive nervousness as when the mouth twitched, for dizziness, and with one herb added for insanity." As an instance of its successful use Gagawin said that a certain woman said someone had threatened to poison her. Gagawin told her to steep this root, keep it in a bottle and drink some occasionally, and if this did not have the desired effect, he would give her something else to take with it. This remedy, however, was sufficient, and she did not return.
(2) _____do_____	The powdered root was put on hot stones. Patient covered his head and inhaled the fumes.	
(3) _____do_____	The powdered root was moistened with lukewarm water and applied to incisions on the temples by means of soft duck down. (See p. 332.)	
(4) Dried_____	Chewed_____	See Nosebleed and charms.
(5) Decoction_____	Internally_____	
Decoction_____	Sprinkled on hot stones and fumes inhaled.	See Eruptions, tonics, and remedies for the horse.
Dried and pulverized _____	Combined with tobacco or red willow, smoked in a pipe, and the smoke inhaled.	See also Charms.
Decoction_____	Sprinkled on hot stones and the smoke inhaled.	
Dried and pulverized_____	"Smelled"_____	See Lung trouble.

³ This root grows straight downward and then turns sharply. The strongest medicinal value is at the elbow where the root turns.

† Plants thus marked are mentioned in the United States Pharmacopœia. (See p. 299.)

System or part affected	Symptoms	Botanical name	Part of plant used
Nervous system........	Convulsions	Hicoria alba. (Hickory.)..........	Small shoots......
Do...............	.....do................	Thuja occidentalis L.† (Arbor vitae.)	Wood............
Do...............	.....do................	Corylus americana Walt. (Hazel.)	Stalk............
Do...............	.....do................	Abies balsamea (L.) Mill.† (Balsam fir.)	Gum............
Do...............	.....do................	Drymocallis arguta (Pursh) Rydb. (Five-finger.)	Root............
Do...............	"Craziness"..........	Vaccinium angustifolium Ait. (Blueberry.)	Flowers..........
Circulatory system.....	Heart................	Petalostemon purpureus (Vent) Rydb. (Prairie clover.)	Leaves and flowers.
Do...............	.....do................	Quercus macrocarpa Muhl. (Bur oak.)	Inner bark........
		Quercus rubra L.† (Red oak)	.....do............
		Populus tremuloides Michx. (Aspen.)	.....do............
		Populus balsamifera L.† (Balsam poplar.)	Equal amounts of root, bud and blossom.
		Polygala senaga L. (Seneca snakeroot.)	Root............
Do...............	Heart palpitation......	Apocynum androsaemilifolium L. (Dogbane.)	....
Do...............	.....do.	Artemesia dracunculoides† Pursh. (flowering plant). (Mugwort.)	(1) Leaves and flowers.
			(2) Leaves........

† Plants thus marked are mentioned in the United States Pharmacopœia. (See p. 299.)

How prepared	How administered	Remarks and references
Fresh _____	Placed on hot stones and fumes inhaled.	The shoots thus used were the very small shoots that grow beside the leaves.
Burned and charcoal used_____	Combined with bear's gall, pricked into the temples with needles.	The manner of administering this is described on p. 333.
_____do_____	Administered as above_____	
No preparation necessary_____	Placed on warm stone until it melts; fumes inhaled.	See Hair.
Dried and pulverized_____	(1) Applied on incisions in the temples (see p. 332). (2) Moistened root inserted in nostrils.	See Dysentery and hemorrhage.
Dried_____	Placed on hot stones and fumes inhaled.	This was said to be one of the remedies given by Winabojo. These remedies are the most highly regarded.
Decoction; handful of leaves and flowers in 1½ pints water.	Dose, ½ cup; repeat in half hour if necessary.	
Scraped and dried; equal parts of this and two next following were powdered in the hands. This medicine was prepared ceremonially. (See tonic remedy similarly prepared, Bull. 63, p. 65.) A pail was made ready containing about a pint of water. A little of the mixed bark was placed on the water at the eastern side, the medicine man saying "Wa′ bûn-oŋg" (eastward); the same was repeated at the south, west, and north with similar words. He then placed on the top of these piles a smaller portion of the powdered Polygala Senegala root, saying the same words. The medicine was then allowed to steep. It was said to be very powerful so that care must be used not to take too much of it. The dose was measured in a small receptacle made of birch bark (pl. 46, h) and marked with a symbol of the remedy, or "one swallow" was taken, the dose being repeated in an hour.	Internally_____	
"Take 4 pieces of the dried root, about 2 inches long. Put in 1 quart of water. Let it come to a boil, and boil about 2 minutes."	A "good drink" of the decoction was taken as often as desired.	The root of this plant was said to grow to a great length, and usually to be found running north and south. A weaker decoction was used as a remedy for earache, and a very weak decoction was said to be good for a baby's cold.
Dried; a handful steeped in 1½ pints of water.	Administered when partly cooled; dose, ½ cup, after which the patient reclined; dose repeated every half hour until patient was relieved.	See Diseases of women, hemorrhages, dysentery, tonics and remedies for the hair.
Fresh_____	Chewed_____	

System or part affected	Symptoms	Botanical name	Part of plant used
Circulatory system ___	"Humor in the blood"	Aralia nudicaulis L.† (Wild sarsaparilla.)	Root_____
Respiratory system____	Colds_____	Acorus calamus L.† (Calamus.)__	_____do_____
Do_____	_____do_____	Allium stellatum Ker. (Wild onion.)	_____do_____
Do_____	_____do_____	Caltha palustris L.† (Cowslip)__	_____do_____
Do_____	_____do_____	Apocynum androsaemifolium L. (Dogbane.)	_____
Do_____	Cough_____	Agastache anethiodora (Nutt.) Britton.† (Giant hyssop.)	_____do_____
Do_____	_____do_____	Apocynum sp. (Dogbane)_____	_____do_____
Do_____	_____do_____	Aralia racemosa L.† (Spikenard)_	_____do_____
Do_____	_____do_____	Arctium minus Bernh.† (Burdock.)	Leaves_____
Do_____	_____do_____	Ceanothus ovatus Desf. (New Jersey tea.)	Root_____
Do_____	_____do_____	Ostrya virginiana (Mill.) Koch.† Hop hornbeam (ironwood).	Wood_____
		Thuja occidentalis L.† (Arbor vitae.)	Leaves_____
Do_____	Lung trouble_____	Caulophyllum thalictroides (L.) Michx.† (Blue cohosh.)	Root_____
Do_____	_____do_____	Euthamia graminifolia (L.) Nutt_ (Goldenrod.)	_____do_____
Do_____	_____do_____	Lonicera sp. (Honeysuckle)_____	_____do_____
Do_____	_____do_____	Rubus frondosus Bigel.(?) (Blackberry.)	_____do_____
		Quercus macrocarpa Muhl. (Bur oak.)	Inner bark_____
Do_____	_____do_____	Silphium perfoliatum L.† (Cupplant.)	Root_____
Do_____	_____do_____	Solidago rigidiuscula Porter.† (Goldenrod.)	_____do_____
		Pulsatilla hirsutissima (Pursh) Britton.† (Pasque-flower.)	_____do_____
Do_____	Hemmorhages from lungs.	Solidago rigidiuscula Porter.† (Goldenrod.)	_____do_____
Do_____	_____do_____	Prunus virginiana L. (Chokecherry.)	Inner bark_____
		Corylus sp. (Hazel)_____	Root_____
		White oak (specimen not obtained).	_____do_____
		Ostrya virginiana (Mill.) Koch. (Ironwood.)	Heart of the wood_

† Plants thus marked are mentioned in the United States Pharmacopœia. (See p. 299.)

How prepared	How administered	Remarks and references
Decoction _____	Internally _____	See Diseases of women and nosebleed.
(1) Pulverized _____	Snuffed up nostrils _____	See Toothache, sore throat, and physic.
(2) Decoction _____	Internally _____	
Decoction, sweetened _____	____do _____	Used chiefly for children.
"Chop 2 roots, boil in scant tea- cup of water; remove from fire when it boils; strain and cool."	Drink entire amount at once. This was said to produce perspiration, loosen phlegm, and act as an emetic. Drink warm water after medicine has acted; repeat five days later. This is usually suf- ficient; it was said that too much was an injury.	This use of the herb was said to be a great secret. See also Scrofula and diseases of women.
Very weak decoction of root _____	Internally _____	Used only for infants.
Steeped _____	____do _____	This was used for an internal cold with tendency to pneumonia, also for pain in chest.
Dried and pulverized _____	Snuffed up nostrils _____	This was used for a heavy cold in the head, and was said to cause sneezing and relieve the head.
Decoction _____	Internally _____	See Boils and fracture.
Infusion; made from a handful of leaves and a teacup of boiling water.	____do _____	This was used for a hard dry cough and taken after a coughing spell.
Decoction; made from 5 inches of root, grated, and 1 quart of water.	Internally. Dose is 1 swal- low.	
These were used with other in- gredients in making a cough sirup.	Internally _____	See Kidney trouble.
Decoction; made from 2 roots and 1 quart water.	Internally. Dose is 1 swal- low.	See Emetics.
Decoction _____	Internally _____	This was said to be particularly good for pain in the chest.
Decoction; with other ingre- dients not designated.	____do _____	
Decoction _____	____do _____	The second named was used for cramps.
____do _____	____do _____	This was used for hemorrhage from the lungs, also for pain in the back and chest with tendency to consumption.
Decoction; made from a double handful of the pulverized roots to 2 quarts of water.	____do _____	
Decoction; made from 1 root and a quart of water.	"Take it cold" _____	This remedy was used to check a sud- den hemorrhage from the lungs. See Pain in back, sprain, diseases of women, and remedies for the hair.
Steeped together _____	Internally _____	

System or part affected	Symptoms	Botanical name	Part of plant used
Digestive system_____	Sore mouth_____	Heuchera (species doubtful). (Alum-root.)	Root_____
		Rhus glabra L.† (Sumac)_____	Blossom cut when white bloom is on.
Do_____	_____do_____	Castalia odorata (Ait.) Woodv. & Wood. (White waterlily.)	Root_____
Do_____	_____do_____	Geranium maculatum L.† (Wild geranium.)	_____do_____
Do_____	Toothache_____	Acorus calamus L.† (Calamus)___	_____do_____
Do_____	_____do_____	Cypripedium hirsutum Mill.† (Ladyslipper.)	_____do_____
Do_____	_____do_____	-------------------------------------	Fungus; it is gathered about middle of August.
Do_____	Sore throat_____	Tanacetum vulgare L.† (Tansy)_	Root_____
Do_____	_____do_____	Heracleum lanatum Michx.† (Cow parsnip.)	_____do_____
Do_____	_____do_____	Solidago flexicaulis L. (Goldenrod)	_____do_____
Do_____	_____do_____	Osmorrhiza claytoni Michx. (Sweet cicely.)	_____do_____
Do_____	_____do_____	Acorus calamus L.(†) (Calamus.)_	_____do_____
Do_____	_____do_____	Phryma leptostachya L. (Lopseed.)	_____do_____
Do_____	_____do_____	Potentilla monspeliensis L. (Cinquefoil.)	Root and stalk____
Do_____	_____do_____	Prunus virginiana L. † (Chokecherry.)	Inner bark_____
Do_____	_____do_____	Zanthoxylum americanum Mill.† (Prickly ash.)	Root_____
Do_____	_____do_____	Ulmus fulva Michx. (Slippery elm.)	(1) Bark_____
			(2) Root_____
Do_____	Indigestion_____	Asarum canadense L. † (Wild ginger.)	_____do_____
Do_____	_____do_____	Sieversia ciliata (Pursh) Rydb. (Prairie smoke.)	_____do_____
		Heuchera (species doubtful). (Alum-root.)	_____do_____
Do_____	_____do_____	Caulophyllum thalictroides (L.) Michx.† (Blue cohosh.)	_____do_____
		Rudbeckia laciniata L.† (Coneflower.)	_____do_____
Do_____	_____do_____	Sagittaria latifolia Willd. (Arrowhead.)	_____do_____
Do_____	_____do_____	Cypripedium hirsutum Mill.† (Ladyslipper.)	_____do_____
Do_____	_____do_____	Salix (species doubtful). (Willow.)	Inner bark_____
Do_____	Pain in stomach_____	Andropogon furcatus Muhl. (Bluestem.)	Root_____
Do_____	_____do_____	Betula nigra. (Black birch)_____	Bark_____
Do_____	_____do_____	Diervilla lonicera Mill. (Bush honeysuckle.)	Leaves_____
Do_____	_____do_____	Erigeron canadensis L. † (Horseweed.)	Root and leaves___

† Plants thus marked are mentioned in the United States Pharmacopœia. (See p. 299.)

How prepared	How administered	Remarks and references
Decoction; made from one root and one blossom in a teacup of water, strained and cooled.	"Put it on something soft and wash the child's mouth."	This was used for the sore mouth of a child when teething, and was said to heal the gums quickly. The first named was used for dysentery. A fungus growing on the latter plant was also used for dysentery.
Dried and finely powdered_____	Put in the mouth_____	
Dried and powdered_____	_____do_____	Used especially for children.
(1) Dried_____	Chewed_____	See Cold; physic and sore throat. This was used for children. See stomach trouble and inflammation of the skin.
(2) Decoction_____	Internally_____	
Dried, powdered, and moistened_	Put on decayed teeth_____	
The top is removed and the soft interior substance dampened and used as a poultice.	Used for toothache or put inside a decayed tooth.	It is said to be so strong that it sometimes draws out the nerve.
(1) Decoction_____	Gargle_____	Also used for fevers and for diseases of women.
(2) Dried_____	Chewed_____	
(1) Decoction_____	Gargle_____	This was used for ulcerated sore throat. See Boils.
(2) Dried_____	Chewed_____	
	_____do_____	
Decoction, or chewed_____		See ulcers.
Decoction for children; chewed root used by adults.	Gargle_____	
Decoction, or chewed_____		
_____do_____		
Decoction_____	Gargle_____	This is said to be very astringent. See Cramps and disinfectants.
_____do_____	Internally, also as a gargle___	This was used for quinzy and swelled or ulcerated throat. See Tonics.
_____do_____	Gargle_____	
Dried_____	Chewed_____	
Combined with many other herbs to increase their action.	Internally_____	If food does not agree with a person, put about an inch of this root in whatever food is being cooked for him. See tonics and inflammation.
A decoction was made from 4 roots of first named, 1 root of second, and 1 quart of water. The first-named root was also used alone in decoction.	_____do_____	This remedy was said to be very strong, so it was taken only occasionally. One preparation was enough to last 2 or 3 days. See Diseases of the horse.
Equal parts of these 2 roots were steeped in water.	_____do_____	Diseases of the horse. Used also for burns.
Steeped_____	_____do_____	This was used if a "person's food did not agree with them."
_____do_____	Internally, given in small doses.	See Toothache and inflammation of skin.
Combined with bark of other trees in decoction.	Internally_____	Do.
Decoction made from 1 root and 1 quart of water.	_____do_____	See Burns and retention of urine.
Decoction_____	_____do_____	
_____do_____	_____do_____	Used only in combinations.
Decoction made from 2 roots and some leaves in 1 quart of water.	_____do_____	

System or part affected	Symptoms	Botanical name	Part of plant used
Digestive system_____	Pain in stomach_____	Heuchera hispida Pursh. (Alum-root).	Root_____
Do_____	_____do_____	Polygonum persicaria L. (Smart-weed.)	Flowers, leaves____
Do_____	_____do_____	Polygonum punctatum Ell. (Smart-weed.)	_____do_____
Do_____	_____do_____	Rhus hirta (L.). Sudw. (Staghorn sumac.)	Flowers_____
Do_____	Colic_____	Stachys palustris L.† (Hedge-nettle.)	Leaves fresh or dry.
Do_____	_____do_____	Thaspium barbinode (Michx.) Nutt. (Meadow parsnip.)	Root_____
Do_____	Cramps_____	Quercus macrocarpa Muhl. (Bur oak.)	_____do_____
Do_____	_____do_____	Viburnum acerifolium L.† (white oak). (Arrowwood.)	Inner bark_____
Do_____	_____do_____	Prunus virginiana L.† (Choke-cherry.)	_____do_____
Do_____	_____do_____	Solidago. (Goldenrod) _____	Root_____
Do_____	_____do_____	Caulophyllum thalictroides (L.) Michx. (Blue cohosh.)	_____do_____
		Sanguinaria canadensis L. (Blood-root.)	_____do_____
Do_____	Dysentery_____	Artemisia dracunculoides Pursh † (flowering plant). (Mugwort.)	Leaves and top__
Do_____	_____do_____	Bursa bursa-pastoris (L.) Britton.† (Shepherd's purse.)	Entire plant_____
Do_____	_____do_____	Urtica gracilis Ait.† (Nettle)____	Root_____
Do_____	_____do_____	Salix (species doubtful). (Willow.)	_____do_____
Do_____	_____do_____	Drymocallis arguta (Pursh) Rydb. (Five-finger.)	_____do_____
		Heuchera (species doubtful). (Alum-root.)	_____do_____
Do_____	_____do_____	Amelanchier canadensis (L.) Medic. (Shadbush.)	_____do_____
Do_____	_____do_____	Potentilla palustris (L.) Scop.† (Marshlocks.)	_____do_____
Do_____	_____do_____	Rhus glabra L.† (Sumac)_____	The portion used is a growth which some-times appears on the tree.
Do_____	_____do_____	Rubus strigosus Michx. (Red raspberry.)	Root_____
Do_____	Physic (use of)_____	Acorus calamus L.† (Calamus) __	_____do_____
Do_____	_____do_____	Celastrus scandens L. (Bitter-sweet.)	_____do_____

† Plants thus marked are mentioned in the United States Pharmacopœia. (See p. 299.)

How prepared	How administered	Remarks and references
Dried------------------------------	"Chew the root and swallow the juice."	See Diseases of the eye.
Decoction, strong medicine, yet 1 sprig not enough for a treatment.	Internally-----------------	Used alone and also in combinations.
Decoction-------------------------	------do----------------------	Used only in combinations.
------do---------------------------	------do----------------------	
"Put leaves in hot water and drink it."	------do----------------------	This is used for sudden colic.
Decoction-------------------------	------do----------------------	This is a child's remedy.
------do---------------------------	------do----------------------	See Lung trouble.
------do---------------------------	------do----------------------	See Emetic.
------do---------------------------	------do----------------------	See Sore throat and disinfectant.
Decoction made from 1 root and 1 quart of water.	Externally, applied hot------	Do.
Decoction made from equal amounts of the two roots.	Internally-----------------	See Lung trouble.
------do---------------------------	------do----------------------	Do.
Dried and steeped---------------	------do----------------------	This was used for chronic dysentery. See Diseases of women, hemorrhages, and remedies for the hair.
Decoction----------------------	------do----------------------	This remedy was used for cramps.
Steeped-------------------------	------do----------------------	See Stoppage of urine.
Used alone and also in combination with other roots.	------do----------------------	See Indigestion and sweat lodge customs.
{ Decoction; the first named root was also used alone in decoction.	} ---do-----------------	{ For other uses of first-named root, see Headache and hemorrhages.
Decoction made from this combined with roots of cherry and young oak.	------do----------------------	See Diseases of women.
Decoction made of ½ root and 1 quart water.	------do----------------------	
Dried and pulverized; decoction--	------do----------------------	This remedy was used for obstinate dysentery. The blossom of same plant was combined with alum root and used as a remedy for the sore mouth of a child when teething. See p. 343.
Decoction----------------------	------do----------------------	
The measure for preparing this root was according to the age of the patient, the measure being the length of the index finger, whether an infant or an adult. This quantity of the root was scalded (not boiled), and taken warm. Dose about a half cupful. Same dosage for all physics.	------do----------------------	See Cold, toothache and sore throat.
Decoction. Used especially for babies.	------do----------------------	See Eruptions.

System or part affected	Symptoms	Botanical name	Part of plant used
Digestive system_____	Physic (use of)_____	Dirca palustris L.† (Moosewood)__	Stalk_____
Do_____	_____do_____	Leptandra virginica (L.) Nutt.† (Culver's-root.)	Root_____
Do_____	_____do_____	Falcata comosa (L.) Kuntze. (Hog peanut.)	_____do_____
Do_____	_____do_____	Prunella vulgaris L. (Selfheal)____	_____do_____
Do_____	_____do_____	Smilax herbacea L. (Carrion-flower.)	_____do_____
Do_____	_____do_____	Symphoricarpos (Snowberry)_____	_____do_____
Do_____	Emetic (use of)_____	Allium tricoccum Ait. (Wild leek)	_____do_____
		Caulophyllum thalictroides (L.) Michx.† (Blue cohosh.)	_____do_____
Do_____	_____do_____	Viburnum acerifolium L.† (Arrow wood.)	Inner bark_____
		Alnus incana (L.) Moench.† (Alder.)	_____do_____
Do_____	_____do_____	Viburnum acerifolium L.† (Arrowwood.)	_____do_____
Do_____	Worms_____	Prunus americana Marsh. (Wild plum.)	Root_____
		Prunus serotina Ehrh.† (Wild cherry.)	_____do_____
Do_____	_____do_____	Monarda mollis L. (Horsemint)_	Root and flowers__
Do_____	Cholera infantum_____	Prunus serotina Ehrh.† (Wild cherry.)	Root_____
Do_____	_____do_____	Fragaria virginiana Duchesne.† (Wild strawberry.)	Roots_____
Urinary system_____	Kidney trouble_____	Smilax herbacea L. (Carrion-flower.)	Root_____
Do_____	_____do_____	Ostrya virginiana (Mill.)† Koch. (Hop hornbeam.)	Wood_____
Do_____	Stoppage of urine_____	Urtica gracilis Ait.† (Nettle)_____	Root_____

† Plants thus marked are mentioned in the United States Pharmacopœia. (See p. 299.)

How prepared	How administered	Remarks and references
"Cut up the stalk and dry it, pulverize, put about a tablespoon in warm water, steep but do not let it boil. Do not eat after taking it. Green stalk may be chewed."	Internally_____	See use of root as a hair wash.
Decoction made of 5 roots and 1 quart of water.	_____do_____	It was said that this physic also "cleansed the blood."
Decoction made of this combined with other roots.	_____do_____	
Decoction, combined with catnip	_____do_____	
Decoction, combined with other roots.	_____do_____	See Kidney trouble.
Decoction made of 2 inches of dried root in a little water.	_____do_____	This was said to be a very strong remedy. See Stoppage of urine.
Decoction, 1 root proper amount for a dose; quick in its effect.	_____do_____	
"Scrape the root fine. Tie a small quantity in a white cloth and squeeze it in warm water."	_____do_____	This is also used as a remedy for biliousness and for hemorrhages from the lungs.
"In preparing these, scrape the stalks carefully, removing only the thin outer covering and using the green part underneath. Put the scrapings of this green bark from both trees in boiling water to make decoction."	_____do_____	
"Break up the bark, put it in a cloth and put the cloth in hot water, squeeze it until the water is green. Let it cool and take it with plenty of water."	_____do_____	See Cramps.
Decoction_____	_____do_____	The first named was also used as a disinfectant wash. The second named was used for ulcers, cholera infantum, and scrofulous neck.
_____do_____	_____do_____	See uses of flowers and leaves for eruptions and burns.
"Boil a handful of the prepared roots in about 1 pint of water."	_____do_____	See Worms, ulcers, and scrofula; also disinfectant wash.
"Steep 2 or 3 roots in 1 quart boiling water. Let the child drink freely until the effect is evident."	_____do_____	
Decoction_____	_____do_____	This remedy was used also for pain in the back. It is an old Mide remedy and the root was always carried in a bag made of bear paws. Such a bag was used only by men holding a high degree in the Midewiwin. The native name means "Bear root."
The wood at the "heart of the branches" was cut in small bits and boiled, making a decoction.	_____do_____	See Cough.
Decoction_____	_____do_____	See Dysentery

System or part affected	Symptoms	Botanical name	Part of plant used
Urinary system_____	Stoppage of urine_____	Athyrium filix-foemina (L.) Roth. † (Lady fern.)	Root_____
		Urtica gracilis Ait. (Nettle)_____	_____do_____
Do_____	_____do_____	Celastrus scandens L.† (Bitter-sweet.)	_____do_____
Do_____	_____do_____	Solidago rigida L.† (Goldenrod)_	_____do_____
Do_____	_____do_____	Andropogon furcatus Muhl. (Bluestem.)	_____do_____
		Symphoricarpos albus (L.) Blake.† (Snowberry.)	_____do_____
Do_____	_____do_____	Caltha palustris L.† (Cowslip)__	Leaves and stalks_
		Ribes sp. (Wild currant)_____	_____do_____
Do_____	Gravel_____	Ribes triste Pall. (Red currant)_	Root and stalk____
Skin_____	Inflammation_____	Plantago major L. † (Plantain)__	(1) Leaves_____
			(2) Root_____
Do_____	_____do_____	Plantago major L.†_____	Root_____
		Asarum canadense L.† (Wild ginger.)	_____do_____
Do_____	_____do_____	Eupatorium maculatum L.† (Joe-Pye-weed.)	_____do_____
Do_____	_____do_____	Cypripedium hirsutum Mill.† (Ladyslipper.)	_____do_____
Do_____	Boils_____	Solidago altissima L. (Golden-rod.)	_____do_____

† Plants thus marked are mentioned in the United States Pharmacopœia. (See p. 299.)

How prepared	How administered	Remarks and references
"Cut the first-named root into bits and take a small handful. The root of the second named has lobes on it. Take 4 of these lobes with the first-named root and boil them up quickly. Use as soon as cool enough to drink."	Internally_____	This is known as a "Winabojo remedy," as it is supposed to have been received from him.
Decoction_____	____do_____	This, like the preceding, is one of the Winabojo remedies, the native name being Winabojo onagic, meaning "Winabojo's intestines." The legend is that Winabojo was once walking on the ice when he heard something rattling behind him. He looked back and saw that his intestines were dragging behind him and part had become frozen to the ice. He broke off part and threw them over a tree, saying, "This shall be for the good of my future relatives."
1 root was steeped with ½-pint of water. Dose was "a swallow occasionally."	____do_____	
Decoction; the first-named could be also used alone.	____do_____	The first-named was also used for pain in the stomach and burns.
Decoction_____	____do_____	The root of the first-named was also used for colds, scrofula, and diseases of women.
Decoction made from 4 plants to 1 quart of water. "Boiled quite a while."	____do_____	
Fresh leaves are best. Spread any grease (bear's grease is best) on the surface of the fresh leaves, apply to the inflamed part and as soon as the leaves become dry or heated renew them. If desired for winter use the leaves should be greased, packed in a pile, and wrapped tightly.	Externally_____	See use as a charm, also rheumatism and bites.
Chop fresh roots, spread on a fresh leaf, and apply as a poultice.	____do_____	
Chop fresh roots, spread on fresh plantain leaf, and apply as a poultice.	____do_____	These two were often chopped together and kept in a wrapping of leather.
Decoction used luke warm as a wash for inflammation of the joints.	____do_____	
Chop dried root or in emergency use fresh root. Do not cook but moisten it and apply as a poultice to any inflammation.	____do_____	See stomach trouble and toothache.
Pulverized root was moistened (not cooked), and applied as a poultice.	____do_____	The flowers of this plant were used for burns.

System or part affected	Symptoms	Botanical name	Part of plant used
Skin	Boils	Heracleum lanatum Michx.† (Cow parsnip.)	(1) Root
			(2) R o o t a n d flowers.
Do	do	Aralia racemosa L.† (Spikenard.)	Root
Do	Sores	Aralia nudicaulis L. (Wild sarsaparilla.)	do
Do	Eruptions	Celastrus scandens L.† (Bittersweet.)	Stalk
Do	do	Rumex obtusifolius L. (Bitter dock.)	Root
Do	do	Erysimum cheiranthoides L. (Wormseed mustard.)	do
Do	do	Achillea millefolium L.† (Yarrow.)	do
Do	do	Monarda mollis L. (Horsemint.)	Flowers and leaves.
Do	do	Rumex crispus L.† (Yellow dock.)	Root
Do	do	Erysimum cheiranthoides L. (Wormseed mustard.)	do
Do	Warts	Lactuca canadensis L.† (Wild lettuce.)	Juice
Do	Hair	Solidago rigidiuscula Porter.† (Goldenrod.)	Either root or stalk.
Do	do	Abies balsamea (L.) Mill.† (Balsam fir.)	Gum
Do	do	Artemisia dracunculoides Pursh† (sterile plant). (Mugwort.)	Root
		Dirca palustris L.† (Moosewood.)	do
Do	do	Prunus virginiana L. (Chokecherry.)	Bark
Wounds	Cuts	Populus tremuloides Michx.† (Aspen.)	do
Do	do	Drymocallis arguta (Pursh) Rydb. (Five-finger.)	Root
Do	do	Rumex crispus L.† (Yellow dock.)	do

† Plants thus marked are mentioned in the United States Pharmacopœia. (See p. 299.)

How prepared	How administered	Remarks and references
Boil root and use as a drawing poultice.	Externally..................	It was said that dried root could be used without cooking. See Sore throat.
Dried root and flowers were pounded together and made into a poultice without boiling.	.....do.....................	
Pounded in a cloth and applied as a poultice.	.....do.....................	This poultice was said to be healing as well as "drawing." See Cough and fracture.
The fresh root was mashed and applied as a poultice.	.....do.....................	Used internally as a remedy for the blood.
Decoction...................	.....do.....................	The root of this plant was used for stoppage of urine.
Steeped....................	.....do.....................	Used especially for children.
Decoction made from one root to 1 quart of water.	.....do.....................	3 or 4 roots may be used.
Decoction..................	.....do.....................	See stimulants, headache and diseases of the horse.
Steeped. "Bathe child with the tea and then rub it with tallow, venison tallow if possible."	.....do.....................	Used especially for children. See Worms, and burns.
Dried and powdered root is moistened, spread on a cloth and applied as a poultice in cases of great itching of the skin and eruptions.	.....do.....................	Used especially for children. See Cuts.
Decoction made from 1 root and 1 quart of water; 3 or 4 roots may be used.	.....do.....................	
"Gather the white liquid which oozes out when the stalk is broken and rub this on the wart."	.....do.....................	This remedy is used only from the fresh plant.
Combined with bear's grease as an ointment.	.....do.....................	See Lung trouble, sprain and diseases of women.
.....do...................	.....do.....................	See Headache.
Decoction..................	Used as wash to strengthen the hair and make it grow.	Concerning the first plant, see Heart stimulant, dysentery, hemorrhages from wounds, tonics and diseases of women. The second plant was also used as a physic.
.....do...................	.....do.....................	
"Spit on the cut and draw the edges together, then chew this bark and apply thickly like a poultice as soon as possible. Dried root may be used in the same manner."	Externally..................	See Diseases of women.
Moisten the dried and pulverized root.	.....do.....................	See Dysentery and headache.
Dried and pounded............	.....do.....................	This was used for a "clean cut." See Eruptions and ulcers.

System or part affected	Symptoms	Botanical name	Part of plant used
Wounds	Cuts	Pinus strobus L. (White pine)	Trunk of young tree.
		Prunus serotina Ehrh.† (Wild cherry.)	Inner bark
		Prunus americana Marsh. (Wild plum.)	Inner bark of young tree.
Do	do	Solidago rigidiuscula Porter.† (Goldenrod.)	Root
Do	Bites of poisonous reptiles.	Lilium canadense L. (Lily)	do
Do	do	Plantago major L.† (Plantain)	Leaves and root
Do	do	Botrychium virginianum (L) Sw. (Rattlesnake fern.)	Root
Bruise		Epilobium angustifolium L. † (Fireweed.)	Leaves
Burns		Agastache anethiodora (Nutt.) Britton. (Giant hyssop.)	(1) Leaves
			(2) Leaves and stalk.
Do		Solidago altissima L. (Goldenrod.)	Flowers
		Rudbeckia laciniata L.† (Coneflower.)	do
		Agastache anethiodora (Nutt.) Britton. (Giant hyssop.)	do
Do		Larix laricina (Du Roi) Koch.† (Tamarack.)	Inner bark

† Plants thus marked are mentioned in the United States Pharmacopœia. (See p. 299.)

How prepared	How administered	Remarks and references
"Cut the first named into sections and boil with the barks until soft, strain, keeping the decoction, pound the woody material into a mash and dry; when needed, soak the mash thoroughly in the decoction and apply; care should be taken that the barks after boiling do not come in contact with rust or dirt."		The informant stated that he used this successfully on a gunshot wound after gangrene had set in. This could be applied to any form of "rotten flesh," after which a knife was used to cleanse the wound.
Decoction made from 1 root and 1 quart of water. Taken cold.	Internal	This remedy is used to check the hemorrhage when a person has been wounded and blood comes from the mouth. See Lung trouble, and diseases of women.
Root used in decoction	Externally	This was also used "when a snake blows on a person and causes a swelling."
Fresh, chopped fine, and applied to bite. This was sometimes spread on a fresh leaf of the plant.	do	An incident of the use of this plant was related. Mrs. Razer had a relative who was bitten by a poisonous snake while picking berries. Her husband put a tight bandage around the arm above the bite; then searched for the plant. Before he could find it the woman's arm was badly swollen. He cut little gashes in the arm, moistened this root, applied it, and the woman's life was saved. See Rheumatism and inflammation.
A poultice of the fresh root, mashed, was applied to a snake bite.	do	"If a snake got into the wigwam a decoction of this root was sprinkled around and the snake did not return."
Fresh or dried leaves were moistened and made in a poultice.	do	The same poultice might be used to remove a sliver.
Dried and powdered leaves moistened with water and applied.	do	This was said to prevent blister and take out the fire. See Colds and charms.
Chew the fresh leaves and stalk. Apply as a poultice.		
A "small sunflower" was combined with these, the flowers being dried and used as a poultice. When needed the flowers were moistened, applied, and covered with a bandage; when this became dry it was not removed but was moistened with cold water.	Externally	The leaves of the last named were used alone for a burn, being dried, powdered, and applied as a poultice. This combination of medicine was very strong and was called Wabuno-wuck (eastern medicine). It is said that if a small handful of flowers of the plants were steeped in a quart of water and a person "washed their hands" in this decoction they could thrust their hands in boiling water and not be scalded. The root of the second plant was used for indigestion. (Cf. Bull. 45, p. 103.)
Fresh or dried, chop fine and apply to burn. Apply in morning, wash off partially at night, and renew.	do	

System or part affected	Symptoms	Botanical name	Part of plant used
Burns		Clintonia borealis (Ait.) Raf. (Clintonia.)	Leaf
Do		Monarda mollis L. (Horsemint)	Flowers and leaves
Ulcers		Solidago altissima L. (Goldenrod.)	Flowers
Do		Prunus serotina Ehrh.† (Wild cherry.)	Root
		Ledum groenlandicum Oeder.† (Labrador tea.)	___do
Do		Prunus (species doubtful)	___do
Do		Rumex crispus L. (Yellow dock)	___do
Do		Osmorrhiza claytoni (Michx.) Britton. (Sweet cicely.)	___do
Fevers		Nepeta cataria L.† (Catnip)	Leaves
Do		Koellia virginiana (L.) Mac M.† (Mountain mint.)	___do
		Nepeta cataria L. (Catnip)	___do
Do		Tanacetum vulgare L.† (Tansy)	___do
		Nepeta cataria L.† (Catnip)	___do
Do		Solidago (species doubtful). (Goldenrod.)	___do
Scrofula	Sores	Leptandra virginica (L.) Nutt.† (Culver's-root.)	Root
		Prunus virginiana L.† (Chokecherry.)	Inner bark
Do	___do	Prunus serotina Ehrh.† (Wild cherry.)	Root or bark
Do	___do	Caltha palustris L.† (Cowslip)	Root
Do	___do	Clintonia borealis Ait. (Clintonia)	Leaves

† Plants thus marked are mentioned in the United States Pharmacopœia. (See p. 299.)

How prepared	How administered	Remarks and references
Fresh_____	Externally_____	
Dried, powdered in the hand, moistened with water and applied to burn.	_____do_____	Especially good for a scald.
Dried, moistened with cold water.	_____do_____	See Boils.
Dried, powdered and mixed, but not cooked. After this powder has been on the flesh for a time it becomes damp. It is then removed, the sore washed, and a fresh application made.	_____do_____	Applied to a severe burn or ulcer or any condition in which the flesh is exposed. Concerning the first-named plant see Cholera infantum, and scrofula.
Decoction of dried root or scraped and mashed fresh root.	_____do_____	See Diseases of women.
Dried and pounded_____	_____do_____	See Cuts and eruptions.
Dried and pounded, moistened with warm water.	_____do_____	Used especially for a running sore.
Decoction_____	Internally_____	
Decoction made from equal parts of leaves of 2 plants. Directions are as follows: "If a person feels chilly he should take 1 cup of this medicine as hot as possible, repeating the dose after a short time. He should also wrap up and go to bed; when the fever comes on he should take the same decoction, but cold and whenever desired."	_____do_____	
Equal quantities of the leaves of these plants were steeped together.	_____do_____	This remedy was used to produce a profuse perspiration and break up a fever. The first root was used also for sore throat and for diseases of women.
Dried and a decoction made_____	_____do_____	
Decoction made from 4 roots of first, a large handful of bark of second, and 1 pint of water. Dose, 1 swallow taken before breakfast and at frequent intervals, usually before eating.	Internally (used with the external remedy which follows).	The action of this remedy is a mild cathartic intended to cleanse the blood.
Use fresh roots mashed as a poultice; or scrape the inner bark, boil, and use water as a wash.	Externally_____	This remedy is especially for scrofulus neck. See Ulcers and cholera infantum.
Dried, powdered and moistened, or fresh root mashed. "Renew the application night and morning."	_____do_____	See Colds and diseases of women.
Decoction_____	_____do_____	

System or part affected	Symptoms	Botanical name	Part of plant used
Hemorrhage	From the nose	Calvatia craniiformis Schw. (Puffball.)	
Do	do	Aralia nudicaulis L.† (Wild sarsaparilla.)	Root
Do	do	Verbena hastata (L.) Morong. (Vervain.)	Flowers
Do	do	Apocynum androsaemifolium L.† (Dogbane.)	Root
Do	From wounds	Tsuga canadensis (L.) Carr.† (Hemlock.)	Inner bark
Do	do	Lathyrus venosus Muhl. (Wild pea.)	Root
Do	do	Quercus (species doubtful). (Oak.)	do
Do	do	Artemisia dracunculoides Pursh. † (Mugwort.)	Leaves and flowers.
Do	do	Rosa arkansana Porter. (Wild rose.)	Root
Do	do	Artemisia frigida Willd. (Prairie sage.)	do
Do	do	Astragalus crassicarpus Nutt. (Ground-plum.)	do
Do	do	Silphium perfoliatum L. (Cupplant.)	Large part of root.
Diseases of women	Female weakness	Amelanchier canadensis (L.) Medic. (Shadbush.)	Bark
Do	do	Erigeron canadensis L. (Horseweed.)	Entire plant
Do	do	Geum canadense Jacq. (Avens).	Root
Do	Pain in back and female weakness.	Cirsium sp.† (Thistle)	do
		Populus balsamifera L.† (Balsam poplar.)	do
Do	do	Crataegus sp. (Thornapple)	do
Do	do	Grossularia oxyacanthoides. (Gooseberry.)	Berry
Do	do	Ribes glandulosum. (Wild currant.)	Root
Do	do	Rubus occidentalis L. (Black raspberry.)	do
Do	do	Vagnera racemosa (L.) Morong. (False Solomonseal.)	do
Do	Stoppage of periods	Artemesia dracunculoids Pursh † (sterile plant). (Mugwort.)	(1) Root
Do	do	do	Root
Do	do	Artemisia dracunculoides Pursh†.	(2) Leaves and stalk.
Do	Difficult labor	do	(3) Leaves, stalk, and root.

† Plants thus marked are mentioned in the United States Pharmacopœia.   (See p. 299.)

How prepared	How administered	Remarks and references
Use soft inner part to plug the nostril, or apply it externally.	Externally_____	
Dried and powdered, or fresh root chewed and inserted in nostril.	_____do_____	See Diseases of women and humor in the blood.
Dried and "snuffed"_____	_____do_____	
Decoction made from 1 arm length and a very little boiling water.	Stuff nostril with cotton moistened with decoction or in severe cases use the mashed root as a plug.	See Headache.
Pulverized and applied dry. This is also used in many combinations.	Externally_____	
Boiled and used as a poultice. Also in a decoction taken internally.	Externally and internally__	This decoction was said to act as an emetic if blood from a wound had accumulated inside patient.
Fresh root chewed, or poultice made from dried root.	Externally_____	For a fresh wound, let it bleed a little before applying poultice.
Fresh or dried, chewed and used as poultice.	_____do_____	See Tonics and diseases of women.
These three were combined with the root of Polygala senega L. in a decoction.	_____do_____	See Fits and tonics.
Dried; cut up and pounded; used as a moist compress.	_____do_____	See Lung trouble and diseases of women.
Decoction, in combination with pin cherry, choke cherry, and wild cherry.	Internally_____	
Steeped_____	_____do_____	
Manner of preparation not stated.	_____	
Decoction made from equal portions of 2 roots, a handful of the roots being used with 1 quart of water; boiled thoroughly. "Take often and freely, about a quart a day."	Internally_____	The buds of second named were used for sprains.
Decoction, in combination_____	_____do_____	
_____do_____	_____do_____	
_____do_____	_____do_____	
_____do_____	_____do_____	
_____do_____	_____do_____	
Decoction made from 8 roots to 1 quart water, all of which could be taken in a day.	_____do_____	Same remedy was used for excessive flowing. This root must be pulled up, not dug. The informant stated this was the only root which must be pulled, not dug.
Another informant stated that she used 4 dried chopped roots in about ¾ cup of water These were not boiled but steeped thoroughly, and the tea taken at frequent intervals.	_____do_____	This remedy was considered so important that its native name is Ogima wuck, meaning "chief medicine."
Decoction, varying in strength according to cases.	_____do_____	
Decoction_____	_____do_____	

System or part affected	Symptoms	Botanical name	Part of plant used
Diseases of women	Stoppage of periods	Koellia virginiana (L.) MacM. † (Mountain mint.)	Root
Do	do	Sanicula canadensis L.† (Bur snakeroot.)	do
Do	do	Ribes triste Pall. (Red currant). Aralia racemosa L.† (Spikenard). Aralia nudicaulis L.† (Wild sarsaparilla.)	Stalk Root do
Do	do	Tanacetum vulgare L.† (Tansy)	Leaves
Do	do	Rubus frondosus Bigel. (Blackberry.)	Root
Do	do	Silphium perfoliatum L.† (Cup-plant.)	do
Do	Excessive flowing	Actaea rubra (Ait.) Willd.† (Red baneberry.)	Root of plant which has white berries.
Do	do	Amelanchier canadensis (L.) Medic. (Shadbush.)	Root
Do	do	Populus tremuloides Michx.† (Aspen.) Populus balsamifera L.† (Balsam poplar.)	do do
Do	Difficult labor	Solidago rigidiuscula Porter.† (Goldenrod.)	do
Do	do	Alnus incana (L.) Moench. (Alder.)	do

† Plants thus marked are mentioned in the United States Pharmacopœia. (See p. 299.)

How prepared	How administered	Remarks and references
Decoction made from a handful of the powdered root and 1 quart of water.	Internally_____	See Tonics and fevers.
Decoction made from a handful of the powdered root and 1 quart of water.	____do_____	
Decoction; the third named was sometimes omitted from this combination. It could also be used alone.	____do_____	This remedy was used if the difficulty threatened to lead to consumption. Concerning the first, see Stoppage of urine, the second, see Boils, cough, and fracture, and the third, "Humors in the blood."
Decoction_____	____do_____	The native name of this plant means young women's drink. In old times the medicines given to maidens were different from those given to married women. This was said to be a rare remedy, and was used as a regulator for young girls. See Fevers and diseases of the ear and throat.
____do_____	____do_____	See Lung trouble.
Decoction; this root was used alone and also as an ingredient in many other remedies of this sort.	____do_____	See Hemorrhages and lung trouble.
Decoction_____	____do_____	There was said to be another variety of this plant which had red berries and was used for diseases of men.
Steeped_____	____do_____	This was given to a pregnant woman who had been injured, to prevent miscarriage.
1 root of each is put in 1 quart of water and is steeped, not boiled. Drink about every hour.	____do_____	This is used for excessive flowing during confinement or to prevent premature birth. The bark of the first named was used for cuts and the buds of the second for sprains.
1 root was steeped in 1 pint of water and taken in 3 doses about 2 hours apart.	____do_____	See Pain in the back, lung trouble, sprain, and remedies for the hair.
In preparing this remedy the root must be scraped upward. A weak decoction is made from a few inches of the root and a pint of water. The following ingredients are added to this: 4 bumblebees are caught and put in a box to die of themselves. In catching the bees they must be stunned but not injured. It destroys the efficacy if the bees are treated otherwise. The bees are dried, ground to a powder, and put in a leather packet until needed. When the medicine is to be used, a pinch of this powder is put in a small half teacup of the above decoction. The dose is about a tablespoonful. Two doses are usually sufficient. A specimen of the bee was obtained and identified as a common bumblebee.	____do_____	The plant is also used for diseases of the eye.

System or part affected	Symptoms	Botanical name	Part of plant used
Diseases of women	Confinement [1]	Caltha palustris L.† (Cowslip)	Root
		Sanicula canadensis L.† (Bur snakeroot.)	do
Do	do	Asclepias syriaca L.† (Common milkweed.)	do
Do	do	Prenanthes alba L. (Rattlesnake root.)	do
Do	do	Cirsium (species doubtful).† (Thistle.)	do
		Taraxacum officinale Weber.† (Dandelion.)	do
Do	Broken breast	Prunus (species doubtful). (Plum.)	do
Disease of eye	Soreness	Arisaema triphyllum (L.) Torr. (Jack-in-the-pulpit.)	do
Do		Chimaphila umbellata (L.) Nutt. (Pipsissiwa.)	do
Do		Cornus alternifolia L.f. † (Dogwood.)	do
Do		Cornus alternifera L. f.†	do
		Cornus stolonifera Michx. (Red-osier dogwood.)	do
		Alnus incana (L.) Moench. (Alder.)	do
Do		Heuchera hispida Pursh. (Alum-root.)	do
Do	Soreness	Stellaria media (L.) Cyrill. †	Leaves
Do	Cataract	Rosa (species doubtful). (Rose)	Inner bark of root
		Rubus strigosus Michx. (Red raspberry.)	do
Do	Sty or inflammation of lid.	Hordeum jubatum L. (Squirrel-tail.)	Root
Do	Sty	Streptopus roseus Michx. (Twist-ed-stalk.)	do
Disease of ear	Soreness	Apocynum androsaemifolium L. (Dogbane.)	do
Do	do	Aster nemoralis Ait. (Aster)	do

[1] A young Chippewa woman whose husband was unable to support a large family said that her mother told her of an herb to prevent childbearing and that she took it. In this connection it is interesting to note that a physician of more than 20 years' experience in the Indian Service told the writer that on all the reservations where he had been stationed he was aware that the Indian women used such an herb and that he had not seen any injurious results from its use.

† Plants thus marked are mentioned in the United States Pharmacopœia. (See p. 299.)

How prepared	How administered	Remarks and references
Decoction_____	Internally_____	The first-named root was used also for colds and scrofula and the leaves and stalk for stoppage of urine.
Take ½ a root, break it up and put it in a pint of boiling water, let it stand and get cold. Whenever the woman takes any liquid food, put a tablespoon of this medicine in the food.	_____do_____	This remedy was used to produce a flow of milk.
Dried and powdered. Was put in the broth a woman drank.	_____	Do.
Take 4 roots of each to one quart of water, steep and use as a drink.	Internally_____	Do.
The dried roots were used in decoction or fresh roots were scraped and mashed.	Externally_____	See Ulcers.
Decoction_____	_____do_____	
_____do_____	Drop in the eye_____	
Scrape and steep the root, using a handful to about a pint and a half of water. Let it cool and strain well.	Bathe the eye and let some of the liquid get into the eye, or use it on a compress.	See Charms.
Decoction made from equal parts of these roots.	As a wash or compress_____	The last named is used also for diseases of women.
Decoction made from whole root.	Externally_____	See Pain in stomach.
Put a handful of the leaves in hot water, do not let it boil long, let it stand and strain it.	Externally (wash)_____	
These two remedies are used successively, the first for removing inflammation, and the second for healing the eye. They are prepared in the same way, the second layer of the root being scraped and put in a bit of cloth. This is soaked in warm water and squeezed over the eye, letting some of the liquid run into the eye. This is done 3 times a day.	_____	It was said that these would cure cataract unless too far advanced, and that improvement would be shown quickly if the case could be materially helped.
Dried, pounded, put in a cloth which was moistened with warm water and sopped on the eye.	Externally_____	This remedy was so strong that one root would have an effect.
Steeped root was used as a poultice.	_____do_____	
Decoction made with about 1 inch of the root	Poured into ear from a spoon.	See remedies for headache.
Decoction_____	Drop in ear or apply on cloth; use lukewarm water.	

System or part affected	Symptoms	Botanical name	Part of plant used
Disease of ear	Soreness	Campanula rotundifolia L. (Harebell.)	Root
Do	___do	Tanacetum vulgare L.† (Tansy)	___do
Do	___do	Trillium grandiflorum (Michx.) Salisb.† (Wake-robin.)	Inner bark of root
Diseases of joints	Rheumatism	Abies balsamea (L.) Mill.† (Balsam fir.)	Root
Do	___do	Anaphalis margaritacea (L.) B. & H. (Pearly everlasting.)	Flowers
Do	___do	Castilleja coccinea (L.) Spreng. (Painted-cup.)	___do
Do	___do	Juniperus virginiana L. (Red cedar.)	Little twigs
Do	___do	Taxus canadensis Marsh. (Yew)	___do
Do	___do	Vitis cordifolia Michx. (Grape)	Root
Do	___do	Trillium grandiflorum (Michx.) Salisb.† (Wake-robin.)	___do
Do	___do	Plantago major L.† (Plantain)	Leaves
Do	___do	Any variety of evergreen	Twigs
Do	___do	Lycopodium obscurum L. (Ground-pine.)	Moss
		Picea canadensis (Mill.) B. S. P. (White spruce.)	Twigs
		Ostrya virginiana (Mill.) Koch. (Ironwood.)	Chips cut from "heart" of the wood.
Do	Sprain or strained muscles.	Artemisia absinthium L.† (Wormwood.)	Entire top of plant.
Do	___do	Solidago rigidiuscula Porter.† (Goldenrod.)	Either stalk or root.
Do	___do	Populus balsamifera L.† (Balsam poplar.)	Buds before they open.
Do	___do	Allionia nyctaginea Michx. (Umbrella-plant.)	Root
Do	___do	Aralia racemosa L.†	___do
Baths		Artemisia dracunculoides Pursh.† (Mugwort.)	Root, the best part was the fine fibers.

† Plants thus marked are mentioned in the United States Pharmacopœia. (See p. 299.)

How prepared	How administered	Remarks and references
Take 1 root to one half cup of water; steep and strain.	Use lukewarm water and drop a very little in the ear.	See Remedies for headache.
Weak decoction_____	Dropped in ear lukewarm___	See Throat, fever and diseases of women.
Scrape the second layer of the bark of the root, put in hot water and boil.	Dropped in the ear_____	See Rheumatism.
Decoction_____	Sprinkled on hot stones, the decoction being very hot. This was used to "steam" rheumatic joints, especially of the knees, the patient being covered closely and letting steam warm the knees. See Headache and remedies for the hair.	
Decoction (steeped)_____	Used in combination with wild mint, sprinkled on hot stones, said to be good for paralysis.	
_____do_____	Used singly or in combination, said to be good for paralysis; also good for a cold.	
These were boiled together_____	Decoction sprinkled on hot stones or taken internally.	The informant, a woman of advanced age, said this remedy came from her great-grandmother.
Steeped_____	Internally_____	See Diabetes in general remedies.
Decoction_____	"Pricked in with needles." (See p. 343.)	See Diseases of the ear.
Prepared and applied as for inflammation.	Externally_____	See Inflammation and bites.
Placed on hot stones_____	Used for steaming rheumatic joints.	
Decoction made from these three.	Used for steaming stiff joints.	
Boiled_____	As a warm compress_____	
_____do_____	_____do_____	This was used especially when a sprain was followed by swelling. See Tonics and remedies for the hair.
(1) Steeped and used as a poultice. (2) Boiled in grease (about a handful of buds to a cup of grease), strained and kept for use when needed. Deer tallow is not good for this purpose, but bear's grease is excellent.	Externally_____	The root of this plant was used for the diseases of women.
Dried root in decoction or fresh root pounded and applied as a poultice.	_____do_____	
_____do_____		
Strong decoction_____	Strengthening bath for a child, also used for "steaming old people to make them stronger."	Various parts of this plant were used for diseases of women, hemorrhages from wounds, and dysentery; also in tonics and a remedy for the hair.

System or part affected	Symptoms	Botanical name	Part of plant used
Baths		Asclepias incarnata L.† (Swamp milkweed.)	Root
Do		Eupatorium maculatum L.† (Joe-Pye-weed.)	____do
Do		Zanthoxylum americanum Mill.†	____do
Tonics and stimulants		Heliopsis scabra Dunal. (Ox-eye)	____do
Do		Sieversia ciliata (Pursh) Rydb. (Prairie-smoke.)	____do
Do		Polygala senega L. (Seneca snake-root.)	____do
		Artemesia frigida Willd. (Prairie sage.)	____do
		Astragalus crassicarpus Nutt. (Ground-plum.)	____do
		Rosa arkansana Porter. (Wild rose.)	____do
Do		Lathyrus venosus Muhl. (Wild pea.)	____do
Do		Fraxinus (species doubtful). (Ash.)	Inner bark
Do		Solidago rigidiuscula Porter.† (Goldenrod.)	Roots and stalks
Do		Achillea millefolium L.† (Yarrow.)	Root
Enemas		Solidago rigida L.† (Goldenrod)	____do
Do		Fraxinus (species doubtful). (Ash.)	____do
Do		Betula papyrifera Marsh. (White birch.)	Inner bark
General remedies	Biliousness	Artemisia frigida Willd. (Prairie sage.)	Leaves
Do	Diabetes	Vitis cordifolia Michx. (Grape)	Root

† Plants thus marked are mentioned in the United States Pharmacopœia. (See p. 299.)

How prepared	How administered	Remarks and references
Put 1 root whole in 1 quart of water, steep, strain, and when cool bathe the child in it. Also good for grown people when sick or tired. Soak feet in it and lie down.	Externally	
Decoction; some of which was put in child's bath.	do	If a child is fretful this will make it go to sleep.
Decoction	do	This bath was used to strengthen legs and feet of a weakly child, especially if the limbs were partly paralyzed. See Tonics and sore throat.
Decoction of dried root or the fresh root chewed and spit on the limbs.	do	This was used to strengthen the limbs.
Dried and chewed	Internally	These roots were chewed before feats of endurance, acting as a strong stimulant. See Indigestion and diseases of the horse.
Dried; the first named is pounded and kept separately. Equal parts of the last three are pounded together until powdered. This medicine is prepared similiarly to that described on page 339. A quart of water is heated and about ⅓ of a teaspoon of the mixed ingredients is placed on the surface of the water at the 4 sides of the pail. A very little of the first (principal ingredient) is placed on top of each. The ingredients soon dissolve. A stronger decoction was secured by boiling. The medicine was taken 4 times a day, the dose being small at first, and gradually increased to about a tablespoonful. A measure made from birch bark was used for this remedy.		The first-named herb could also be taken dry as a tonic. (See Bull. 53, p. 64.)
Decoction	Internally	One dose of this had no effect, results being obtained only by considerable quantity of the remedy.
do	do	See Enema.
do	do	See Lung trouble, sprains, diseases of women, pain in back, and remedies for the hair.
Dried, chewed, and spit on the limbs.	Externally	See Headache, eruptions, and diseases of the horse.
Decoction made from a handful of the root.		See Stoppage of urine.
do		See Tonics.
Steeped		
(1) Burned and vapors inhaled		
(2) Decoction	Internally	
Steeped	do	See Rheumatism.

System or part affected	Symptoms	Botanical name	Part of plant used
General remedies _____	Fracture_____	Asarum canadense L.† (Wild ginger.)	Root_____
		Aralia racemosa L.† (Spikenard)_	_____do_____
Do_____	____do_____	Aralia racemosa L.†_____	_____do_____
Do_____	Swelling_____	Iris versicolor. (Blueflag)_____	_____do_____
Do_____	____do_____	Rumex crispus L. (Yellow dock)_	_____do_____
Do_____	Disinfectant_____	Equisetum hiemale L. (Scouring-rush.)	Leaves_____
Do_____	____do_____	Prunus americana Marsh. (Wild plum.)	Bark_____
Do_____	____do_____	Artemisia frigida Willd. (Sage)__	Leaves_____
Do_____	____do_____	Prunus virginiana L.† (Choke-cherry.)	Inner bark_____
		Amelanchier canadensis (L.) Medic. (Shadbush.)	_____do_____
		Prunus americana Marsh. (Wild plum.)	_____do_____
		Prunus serotina Ehrh.† (Wild cherry.)	_____do_____
Do_____	Antidote for "Bad medicine."	Artemisia gnaphalodes Nutt. (White mugwort.)	Flowers_____
Diseases of the horse___	_____	Psoralea argophylla Pursh.† (Psoralea.)	Root_____
		Aralia nudicaulis L.† (Wild sar-saparilla.)	_____do_____
Do_____	_____	Rudbeckia laciniata L.† (Cone-flower.)	_____do_____
Do_____	_____	Achillea millefolium L.† (Yar-row.)	Leaves and stalk__
Do_____	_____	Laciniaria scariosa (L.) Kuntze. (Blazing-star.)	Root_____
Do_____	_____	Sieversia ciliata (Pursh) Rydb. (Prairie-smoke.)	_____do_____

How prepared	How administered	Remarks and references
Dried and equal parts used; mashed and applied as a poultice. If the arm is very sore and the poultice has become dry the poultice may be moistened with warm water before removing.	Externally...............	The first named used also for indigestion, inflammation, and for tonic and food. The second named used for boils ,cough, and diseases of women.
Decoction................	.....do................	
Poultice; said to be very strong..	......do...............	
Poultice, less strong than preceding, but would cure a swelling in one day if there were no suppuration.	.....do................	
Burned................	....	
Decoction................	Wash...............	
(1) Dried, crumbled, and placed on a hot stone.	Hold the hands and head over it so the fumes get thoroughly into the clothing.	The necessary quantity was said to be "about as much as 4 willow leaves." This was used frequently in cases of contagious disease, the smoke filling the room.
(2) Fresh leaves...............	Stuffed in nostrils and held in the mouth.	This herb was thus used as a protection by a person "working over the dead."
Decoction................	Wash...............	The first was used for gargle and cramps; second, for dysentery and diseases of women, the third for worms, and the fourth for ulcers, cholera infantum, scrofula, and worms.
Dried and placed on coals.......	....	Fumes acted as antidote.
Chopped and steeped with other herbs.	Externally...............	When a horse gives out and is ready to drop, apply this decoction liberally to chest and legs; the second-named plant is used also for nosebleed, humors in the blood and diseases of women.
.....do................	.....do...............	Do. (See Indigestion.)
Decoction................	.....do...............	Used as a stimulant. See Headache, eruptions, and tonics.
Decoction made from 1 root and 1 pint of water.	Externally and internally...	This was given to a horse before a race, and also sprinkled on his chest and legs.
Dried and powdered...............	Put in a horse's feed.........	This was used before a race so the horse would not get winded. See Indigestion and tonics.

Works Containing Lists of Plants Used Medicinally

DENSMORE, FRANCES. Chippewa Music—II. Bull. 53, Bur. Amer. Ethn., 1913, p. 64.

——. Teton Sioux Music. Bull. 61, Bur. Amer. Ethn., 1918, p. 271.

GILMORE, MELVIN R. Uses of plants by the Indians of the Missouri River Region. Thirty-third Ann. Rept. Bur. Amer. Ethn., 1919, pp. 43–154.

HOFFMAN, W. J. The Midewiwin or "Grand Medicine Society" of the Ojibwa. Seventh Ann. Rept. Bur. Ethn., 1891, pp. 197–201, 226, 241, 242.

HUNTER, JOHN D. Memoirs of a Captivity among the Indians of North America. London, 1823. Chapter on "Observations on the Materia Medica of the Indians," with numerous names of plants, pp. 401–447.

MOONEY, JAMES. The Sacred Formulas of the Cherokees. Seventh Ann. Rept. Bur. Ethn., 1891, pp. 324–328.

ROBBINS, W. W., HARRINGTON, J. P., and FREIRE-MARRECO, BARBARA. Ethnobotany of the Tewa Indians. Bull. 55, Bur. Amer. Ethn., 1916.

SMITH, HURON H. Ethnobotany of the Menomini Indians. Bulletin Public Museum of the City of Milwaukee, vol. 4, 1923.

SPECK, FRANK G. Medicine Practices of the Northeastern Algonquians. Proceedings Nineteenth International Congress of Americanists, Washington, 1917, pp. 303–321.

STEVENSON, MATILDA COXE. The Zuñi Indians. Twenty-third Ann. Rept. Bur. Amer. Ethn., 1904, pp. 384–392. (No plant lists.)

SWANTON, JOHN R. Religious beliefs and medical practices of the Creek Indians. Forty-second Ann. Rept. Bur. Amer. Ethn., 1927, pp. 639–670.

PLANTS USED IN DYES

PROCESS OF DYEING

The general process of dyeing among the Chippewa consisted in the use of a vegetable substance to secure a color and of a mineral substance to "set" it. Porcupine quills were the articles most easily dyed, and they retain their color longest. Rushes are the hardest material to dye and often require several "dippings" before the desired shade can be procured. Yarn and ravelings of blankets were among the materials most frequently colored by the Chippewa women. Wooden implements were colored by rubbing them with the fresh root of the blood-root, producing an orange shade.

Both plants and tree products were used in dyes. The latter could be obtained at any season of the year, and the trees used were common trees, so they were usually obtained when needed. An exception is the butternut tree, which does not grow in all parts of the Chippewa country. The inner bark of this is used for black dye, and packets of it are taken from one locality to another and kept as carefully as medicinal roots. Whenever a woman sees a plant that she may at some time need in making dye she gathers it, dries it, and stores it for use.

LIST OF PLANTS USED IN DYES

Botanical name	Common name	Part of plant used
Alnus incana (L.) Moench	Alder	Inner bark.
Betula papyrifera Marsh	White birch	Do.
Coptis trifolia (L.) Salisb	Goldthread	Root.
Cornus stolonifera Michx	Red-osier dogwood	Inner bark.
Corylus americana Walt	Hazel	Green bur.
Juglans cinerea L	Butternut	Bark and root.
Acer	Maple (any variety)	Rotted wood.
Juniperus virginiana L	Cedar	Inner bark.
Lithospermum carolinense (Walt) MacM.	Puccoon	Dried root.
Prunus americana Marsh	Chokecherry	Inner bark.
Quercus macrocarpa Muhl	Bur oak	Do.
Rhus glabra L	Sumac	Pulp of stalk, also inner bark.
Sanguinaria canadensis L	Bloodroot	Inner bark.
Tsuga canadensis (L.) Carr	Hemlock	Do.

MINERAL SUBSTANCES USED IN DYES

The reddish substance that rose to the surface of certain springs was collected, dried, and baked in the fire. It then "became hard like stone." This was powdered and the fine red powder kept in buckskin. When mixed with grease it made a paint that was reddish but not vermilion and was used on arrows and for painting faces and bodies. The "scum" contained iron oxide, and the powder is referred to as ochre in the following formulae.

A black earth which "bubbled up in certain springs" was used in black dyes. The writer visited such a spring on the Manitou Rapids Reserve in Ontario and was told that the Chippewa women buried their rushes in the black earth for a few days and thus secured a satisfactory black color. A specimen of this mud was obtained and submitted to a chemist in Washington who stated that "it is full of compounds of iron with organic acids." He suggested that the method of staining is the action of these irons on the tannin in the wood, producing an ink.

It is said that the material used in earliest times to "set a color" was obtained by putting a piece of "black oak" in "dead water" and allowing it to remain for about two years. Thus it became so hard that it could be used as a whetstone, and the dust from this whetstone was combined with vegetable matter in dyes. At the present time the substance commonly used to "set the color" is the dust from an ordinary grindstone. A specimen of this dust was submitted to Dr. G. P. Merrill, of the United States National Museum at Washington, who pronounced it silt. On testing it with hydrochloric acid a greenish color was produced, showing the presence of iron.

FORMULAE FOR DYES [1]

RED DYE

FIRST FORMULA

Betula papyrifera Marsh. White birch.
Cornus stolonifera Michx. Red-osier dogwood. Outer and inner bark.
Quercus species. Oak.
Ashes from cedar bark.
Hot water.

Directions.—Boil the barks in the hot water. Prepare the ashes by burning about an armful of scraps of cedar bark. This should make about 2 cups of ashes, which is the correct quantity for about 2 gallons of dye. Sift the ashes through a piece of cheesecloth. Put them into the dye after it has boiled a while, then let it boil up again, and then put in the material to be colored. Do not let a man or any outsider look into the dye.

---

[1] Unless otherwise stated, the portion of the tree used in dye was the inner bark.

Lithospermum carolinense (Walt) MacM. Puccoon. Nine inches of the dried root or an equivalent amount of the pulverized root.
Hot water, 1 quart.
Ochre, 1 teaspoonful.

Directions.—If this is being used for dyeing porcupine quills, let it boil up a little, then put in the quills, which have previously stood for a while in hot water. Let the quills boil half an hour to an hour, keeping the kettle covered, then remove from the fire and let the quills stand in the dye for several hours. If they are not bright enough they may be redyed, letting them stand in the dye as before. The process is substantially the same in dyeing other materials.

This formula was used by Mrs. Razer in dyeing porcupine quills for the writer, the result being a brilliant scarlet which closely resembled analine dye. The quills were seen in the dye.

Sanguinaria canadensis L. Bloodroot. 2 handfuls. Root.
Prunus americana Marsh. Wild plum. 1 handful.
Cornus stolonifera Michx. Red-osier dogwood. 1 handful.
Alnus incana (L.) Moench. Alder. 1 handful.
Hot water, 1 quart.

The inner bark of the trees and the root of the bloodroot were used, all being boiled before the quills were put in the dye.

Sanguinaria canadensis L. Bloodroot. 1 handful. Root.
Prunus americana Marsh. Wild plum. 1 handful.
Hot water, 1 quart.

Tsuga canadensis (L.) Carr. Hemlock. Bark.
A little grindstone dust.
Hot water.

Juniperus virginiana L. Red cedar.

The bark of this tree was used by Chippewa women in Ontario for coloring the strips of cedar used in their mats. A decoction was made of the dark red inner bark and the strips were boiled in it.

The following formula was used by Mrs. Razer in coloring pieces of white blanket for the writer. The resultant color was a pretty light red. The piece of blanket was exposed to the weather for several weeks and showed slight change of color.

> *Cornus stolonifera* Michx. Red-osier dogwood.
> *Alnus incana* (L.) Moench. Alder.
> Hot water.

The bark of these trees was used in equal parts.

BLACK DYE

The black rushes in the mat illustrated in Plate 48, *a*, were colored with the first of these formulae. It was necessary to dip rushes every day for about two weeks, boiling them a short time and then hanging them up to dry. These rushes are a clear, heavy black. When the process was completed and the black rushes were dry they were rubbed thoroughly with a little lard "to make them shiny and limber."

FIRST FORMULA

> *Juglans cinerea* L. Butternut.
> *Corylus americana* Walt. Hazel, green.

These two were boiled together.

SECOND FORMULA

> *Quercus macrocarpa* Muhl. Bur oak.
> *Juglans cinerea* L. Butternut. Inner bark and a little of the root.
> Black earth.
> Ochre.
> Hot water.

Directions.—Boil the barks and root; after a while put in the black earth and later add the ochre. The more it is "boiled down" the blacker will be the dye. It can be kept in a kettle and heated when used.

THIRD FORMULA

> *Alnus incana* (L.) Moench. Alder.
> *Cornus stolonifera* Michx. Red-osier dogwood.
> *Quercus* species. Oak.
> Either grindstone dust or black earth.
> Hot water.

FOURTH FORMULA

> *Quercus macrocarpa* Muhl. Bur oak.
> *Corylus americana* Walt. Hazel. Green-burs.
> *Juglans cinerea* L. Butternut.
> Black earth.
> Hot water.

Directions.—Put the inner bark of the oak and the green hazel burs in hot water and boil; add other ingredients later. Let it stand a long time before using.

FIFTH FORMULA

Juglans cinerea L.   Butternut.
Grindstone dust.
Hot water.

SIXTH FORMULA

Black earth.
Grindstone dust.

SEVENTH FORMULA

The following formula was used in dyeing a piece of white blanket for the writer. The result was not a heavy black, but this was said to be due to the insufficient quantity of the dye.

Inner bark of oak.
Green hazel burs.
Grindstone dust.
A little ochre dust.
Hot water.

YELLOW DYE

The simplest Chippewa dye is in shades of yellow, as the materials for these shades are easily available and often one substance is sufficient.

FIRST FORMULA

Used in coloring yarn a light yellow, the process being seen by the writer.

Alnus incana (L.) Moench.   Alder.
Hot water.

Directions.—It is best to use only the inner bark, though both inner and outer bark can be used. Either green or dried bark can be used. Pound the bark until it is in shreds and steep it, putting in the material while the dye is hot and letting it boil up. Nothing is needed to set the color.

SECOND FORMULA (LIGHT YELLOW)

Rhus glabra L.   Sumac.   Pulp of the stalk.
Ochre dust (this may be omitted).
Hot water.

THIRD FORMULA (DARK YELLOW)

Sanguinaria canadensis L.   Bloodroot.   Root.
Hot water.

Either the green or dried root is pounded and steeped. Nothing is needed to set the color.

FOURTH FORMULA (DARK YELLOW)

Sanguinaria canadensis L.   Bloodroot.   Double handful of shredded root.
Prunus americana Marsh.   Wild plum.   Single handful of shredded root.
Hot water.

Boil these together.

FIFTH FORMULA (BRIGHT YELLOW)

Coptis trifolia (L) Salisb.   Goldthread.   Roots.
Hot water.

This plant has long slender roots and a great many were required. As in other formulæ, the material was boiled in the dye.

SIXTH FORMULA

Rhus glabra L.   Sumac.   Inner bark.
Sanguinaria canadensis L.   Bloodroot.   Root.
Prunus americana Marsh.   Wild plum.   Inner bark.
Hot water.

The inner bark of the plum was scraped, and it was said that this was used "to set the color."

SEVENTH FORMULA

The formula next following was used in coloring a piece of white blanket for the writer, and produced an ecru or "khaki" color. The piece of blanket was exposed to the weather for several weeks and showed no change in color.

Sanguinaria canadensis L.   Bloodroot.
Prunus americana Marsh.   Wild plum.
Cornus stolonifera Michx.   Alder.
Hot water.

PURPLE DYE

The material used to secure this color is rotten maple wood. It is difficult to obtain, as the wood must be very old.

Rotten maple, double handful.
Grindstone dust, single handful.
Hot water.

The material is boiled in the dye, as in other colors.

GREEN DYE

The Chippewa in Minnesota do not color green with native dyes but a birch-bark basket decorated with dried grass in a bright green color was obtained in Ontario. The Chippewa woman who colored it said that she used green dye, one plant ingredient in the dye being obtained. It was impossible at that season of the year to obtain the principal ingredient.

PLANTS USED AS CHARMS

It was the belief of the Chippewa that many herbs, as well as other substances, possessed the power to act without material contact, affecting the actions or conditions of human beings and animals. In order to make these substances effective it was considered necessary to "talk and pray" over them when they were used, and, in the case of an herb, to "talk and pray" when it was gathered. The Chippewa refer to all such substances or combinations of substances as "medicine," indicating a belief in their extraordinary power. Thus it is said that a man "carries a great many medicines," or "uses medicine all the time," meaning that he has in his possession a large number of materials, probably in little buckskin packets, with which he can produce such effects as safety on a journey, the loss or winning of a race, or the finding of lost articles; or he can cause starvation in a certain lodge, insanity in an individual, or enable a man to bewitch another man's wife. It is said that "the Chippewa were greater medicine people than most of the Indians," the knowledge and use of such substances being transmitted in the Midewiwin together with remedies for treating the sick.

The term "charm" used in this chapter has no Chippewa equivalent. Songs were not used with the working of these charms, the efficacy being secured, as indicated, by "talking and praying." With the "Song of the fire charm" (Bull. 45, Bur. Amer. Ethn., No. 86) a decoction of herbs was applied to the feet, enabling a man to walk in fire without harm. A similar use of herbs, in the present work, is classified as a remedy for burns on page 353.

Charms are considered in the following classes: Love charms, charms to attract worldly goods, charms to insure safety and success, charms to influence or attract animals, charms to work evil, and protective charms. In some instances the charm was carried by the individual working the magic, and in other instances the material was applied to articles belonging to the person who was to be affected by the charm. Herbs were used alone or together with substances believed to increase their power.

Attention is directed to the use of certain plants as charms and also as medicines. A large proportion of the plants used as charms had some value as either medicines or food, but the following are of special interest as the condition supposed to be affected by the charm, and the ailment for which the plant was administered, are alike connected with a disturbance of the nervous system.

Dogbane was used as a protective charm against evil influence or "bad medicine," and also as a remedy for headache.

Wild pea was used as a charm to insure success, especially when the person was in extreme anxiety concerning the outcome of circumstances. It was also used as a remedy for convulsions.

Seneca snakeroot was used as a charm for safety on a journey, which in the minds of the old Indians was attended with some anxiety. It was also used as a stimulating tonic.

LIST OF PLANTS USED IN CHARMS

Botanical name	Part of plant used	Manner of use
Acorus calamus L_____	Root combined with Aralia nudicaulis L.	(1) Decoction made from roots put on fish nets. (2) Decoction used "to rattle snakes away."
Agastache anethiodora(Nutt.) Britton.	Whole plant_____	Protection.
Apocynum androsaemifolium L.	Root_____	Chewed to counteract evil charms.
Aralia nudicaulis L_____	Root combined with Acorus calamus.	
Arctostaphylos uva-ursi (L.) Spreng.	Root_____	Smoked in pipe to attract game.
Artemisia gnaphalodes Nutt_	Flowers dried_____	Placed on coals; fumes as antidote to bad medicine.
Asclepias syriaca L_____	Root combined with root fibers of Eupatorium perfoliatum L.	Applied to whistle for calling deer.
Aster novae-angliae L_____	Root_____	Smoked in pipe to attract game.
Aster puniceus L_____	Fine tendrils of root__	Smoked with tobacco to attract game.
Cornus alternifolia L. f_____	Root_____	Put on muskrat trap.
Eupatorium perfoliatum L__	Root fibers combined with Asclepias syriaca L.	Applied to whistle for calling deer.
Hepatica triloba L_____	Root_____	Put on traps for fur-bearing animals.
Lathyrus venosus Muhl_____	Root dried_____	Carried on the person to insure successful outcome of difficulties.
Onosmodium hispidissimum Mackenzie.	Seeds_____	Love charm; also to attract money or worldly goods.
Plantago major L_____	Root powdered_____	Carried on the person as protection against snake bites.
Polygala senega L_____	Root_____	Carried on person for general health and for safety on a journey.

PLANTS IN USEFUL AND DECORATIVE ARTS

The collection of every tree and plant that entered into the economic life of the Chippewa is not necessary to the present undertaking. The following list is representative, and the familiar quality of many materials is suggestive of their use. Thus, the maple, oak, ash, basswood, ironwood, and pine are so manifestly adapted for the making of household articles, snowshoe frames, sleds, etc., that a detailed account of their use is unnecessary. Brief notations are therefore given concerning the more familiar trees and plants, especially noting the uses which are peculiar to the Indians.

LIST OF PLANTS IN USEFUL AND DECORATIVE ARTS

Botanical name	Common name	Use
Acer saccharum Marsh_____	Maple_____	Paddles for stirring maple sap, etc.
Allium stellatum Ker_____	Wild onion_____	Toys.
Arctium minus Bernh_____	Burdock_____	Leaves for head covering.
Arctostaphylos uva-ursi (L.) Spreng.	Bearberry_____	Smoking.
Betula papyrifera Marsh____	White birch_____	Utensils, coverings for dwellings, patterns for work in decorative art.
Bovista pila B. and C_____	_____	Paint for the dead.
Cicuta maculata L_____	Poison hemlock___	Seeds mixed with tobacco and smoked.
Clintonia borealis Ait_____	Clintonia_____	Patterns bitten in leaves for entertainment.
Cornus rugosa Lam_____	Dogwood_____	Smoking.
Cornus stolonifera Michx____	Red-osier dogwood_	Do.
Corylus americana Walt_____	Hazel_____	Drumming sticks, etc.
Corylus rostrata Ait_____	____do_____	Do.
Crataegus sp_____	Thornapple_____	Thorns used as awls.
Dicranum bonjeanii De Not_	Woodmoss_____	Absorbent.
Equisetum hiemale L_____	Scouring rush_____	Scouring.
Fraxinus sp_____	Ash_____	Making of snowshoe frames, sleds, etc.
Fraxinus nigra Marsh_____	Black ash_____	Bark used in covering wigwams.
Hicoria alba (L.) Britton____	Hickory_____	Bows, etc.
Juniperus virginiana L_____	Red cedar_____	Mats, etc.
Larix laricina (Du Roi) Koch.	Tamarack_____	Roots in weaving bags, etc.
Lithospermum carolinense (Walt) MacM.	Puccoon_____	Face paint.
Ostrya virginiana (Mill.) Koch.	Ironwood_____	Frames for dwelling, etc.
Picea rubra (Du Roi) Dietr_	Spruce_____	Gum used in making pitch, roots in sewing canoes, etc.

Botanical name	Common name	Use
Phragmites communis Trin__	Reed_____	Woven frames for drying berries.
Pinus sp_____	Pine_____	General utility.
Pinus resinosa Ait_____	Red pine_____	General utility and toys.
Quercus sp_____	Oak_____	Awls, etc.
Salix sp_____	Willow_____	Smoking and general utility.
Sarracenia purpurea L_____	Pitcher plant_____	Toys.
Scirpus validus Vahl_____	Bulrush_____	Mats and toys.
Sphagnum_____	Moss_____	Absorbent.
Tilia americana L_____	Basswood_____	Twine and general utility.
Torresia odorata (L.) Hitchc_	Sweet grass_____	Ceremonial, economic and pleasurable.
Typha latifolia L_____	Cat-tail_____	Mats, baskets, etc.
Ulmus fulva Michx_____	Slippery elm_____	General utility.
Urticastrum divaricatum (L.) Kuntze.	False nettle_____	Twine.
	Grass_____	Toys.

MANNER OF USE

Twine was one of the most important articles in the economic life of the Chippewa. It was made chiefly from the inner bark (fiber) of the basswood, though slippery elm bark was also used for this purpose. The twine was used in the weaving of mats and the tying of large and small packets. For some purposes the fiber was used without twisting, the width of the fiber depending on the strength required; thus a strip of fiber as soft and fine as cotton string could be obtained, or a heavy fiber that would hold a considerable weight. The fiber was boiled to give additional toughness if this was especially desired. In preparing the fiber it was customary to cut the bark from the basswood tree in long strips, put it in the water at the edge of a lake, among the rushes, for a few days, after which the soft inner bark could be separated from the outer bark. (Pl. 47.) The fiber thus obtained was separated into strips less than an inch wide and stored in large coils until needed. The twisting of the fiber into twine could be done at any time. Twine was also made from the dry stalks of the false nettle. This was used in sewing and, in two grades of fineness, was used in making fish nets. It is said that a cloth was once made of this fiber and used for women's dresses.

The thorns of the thorn-apple tree were gathered by the women and used as awls in their sewing. Awls were also made of oak.

Bulrush mats for the floor were woven on frames, the basswood twine being passed "over and under" the rushes. (Pl. 48, *a.*) Reeds were used in making the frames on which berries were dried, the stiff, clean *Phragmites communis* being used for this purpose. It was desirable that rushes, bark and similar materials be kept somewhat moist, and a dark, cool shed was adapted to this purpose. Pl. 48, *c*.)

The leaves of the bearberry and the inner bark of red-osier dogwood were smoked for pleasure. (Pl. 49.) The plants smoked as charms are noted in the section on that subject.

Coverings for dwellings were made of sheets of birch bark sewed together with basswood twine, these being used on the dome-shaped wigwam. Sheets of jack pine or of elm were used on the dwellings shaped like the white man's cabin. Cedar boughs were used for bedding. The leaves of the burdock were sewed together or sewed on a strip of birch bark as a head covering for those obliged to work in the hot sun. (Pl. 50, *a*.) The juice of puccoon was used as a paint for reddening the cheeks. A brown fungus (*Bovista pila* B. and C.) was used in painting the faces and garments of the dead, preparatory to their joining the dance of the spirits where the Northern Lights are shining. The flaring lights in the north were said to be the motion of the spirits in their dance, and a woman in a trance saw the spirits paint their faces with this material.

Spruce gum was considered best for use in calking canoes and birch-bark pails. It was prepared by boiling the gum in a wide-meshed bag which retained the bits of wood and bark, allowing the gum to pass into the water. It was skimmed from the surface and stored until a convenient time when it was mixed with charcoal made from cedar. Slippery elm bark was chewed and used occasionally to calk small containers made of birch bark.

Tamarack roots were used in sewing the edges of canoes and in making woven bags.

Rushes were tied in small bundles and used for scouring utensils, the two varieties thus used being *Equisetum hiemale* L. and *Equisetum praealtum* Raf.

Toys were made for children from many sorts of plants. The children themselves cut the stems of the wild onion and made little whistles. The stem, or "top," was allowed to dry a little and a sound hole was cut in the side, after which a sound was produced by blowing across the end. The leaves of the pitcher plant were called "frog-leggings" and used as toys, or filled with ripe berries. Red berries were strung and used as necklaces. Dolls were made from the broad leaves of trees, the leaves being fastened in place with little wooden splints and sometimes a collar of birchbark added. (Pl. 50, *b*.) Flat dolls were cut from the stiff inner bark of slippery elm, or formed of twigs covered with the same sort of willow used for baskets. Dolls were also made of grass. It is interesting to note the lengthened proportions of these dolls and the small bodies which were well adapted to the grasp of a little hand. This was the more advantageous among a people who moved frequently from one camp to another. In these migrations it was necessary for a child to keep possession of its own toys.

The outer covering of cat-tail rushes was formed into toys representing human beings and ducks. (Pl. 51, *a*.) The latter were usually made in groups of five. They were placed on the surface of smooth water, and the child agitated the water by blowing across it, which caused the ducks to move in a lifelike manner.

Little figures were made of tufts of the needles of the red pine or " Norway pine," by cutting across the needles at different lengths to represent the arms and the hem of the dress. (Pl. 51, *b*.) These little figures were placed upright on a sheet of birchbark or, better, on a piece of tin, which was gently agitated in such a manner that the figures appeared to dance. Considerable skill could be shown in producing a motion of the figures.

Grass was used in the making of dolls, as noted, and also in the making of a game implement. The purpose of the game was to toss up the little bundle of grass and catch it on the pointed stick. In the "ring and awl" game the ring was of wood. Numerous other toys and game implements were made of wood.

A "coaster" was made of slippery elm bark (pl. 52, *a*), a stiff piece of bark being selected, turned up at the end, and a piece of stout twine attached to this portion. A child stood on this with one foot, held the twine in its hand, and coasted down hills in winter.

The down of the cat-tail rushes was put around an infant in its cradle board, and sometimes put inside a child's moccasins for additional warmth in winter. Sometimes it was mixed with moss for added warmth.

Three types of uses of sweet grass were noted among the Chippewa—i. e., ceremonial, economic, and pleasurable.

An instance of the first use occurs in the narrative of a hunting incident in which a party of men placed sweet grass on the fire when the camp was in danger of starving and they were going again to hunt. The use of incense is more characteristic of the Plains Indians than of Algonquian tribes.[10]

Medicine men kept sweet grass in the bag with their medicinal roots and herbs.

Strands of sweet grass were made into "coiled basketry" by means of cotton thread. This took the form of bowls, oval and round, and of flat mats. Birch bark was sometimes used as the center of such articles, the coils of sweet grass being sewed around it.

---

[10] See Handbook of American Indians, Bull. 30, Bur. Amer. Ethn., pt. 1, p. 604.

a, TAKING BASSWOOD BARK FROM WATER

b, COILS OF BASSWOOD FIBER

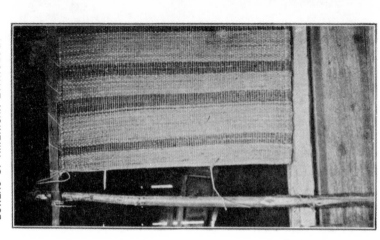

a, RUSH MAT IN FRAME

b, WOMAN CARRYING PACK OF BIRCH BARK

c, STORAGE SHED (OPEN)

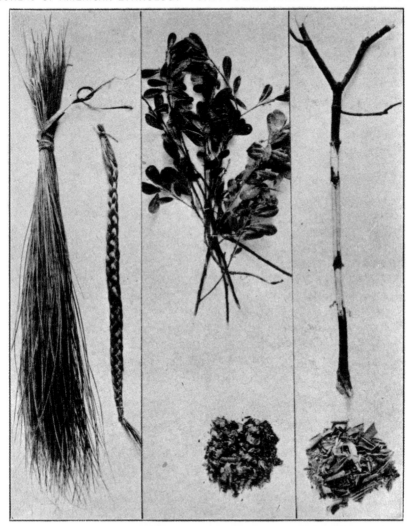

SWEET GRASS AND MATERIALS SMOKED IN PIPE, IN NATURAL
AND PREPARED FORMS

a, HEADBAND OF LEAVES AND BIRCH BARK

b, DOLL MADE OF LEAVES

a, TOYS MADE OF CAT-TAILS

b, DOLLS MADE OF PINE NEEDLES

a, "COASTER" MADE OF SLIPPERY ELM BARK

b, BIRCH BARK SHOWING "PICTURE OF THUNDERBIRD"

c, FIGURES CUT FROM BIRCH BARK

Young people, chiefly young men, carried a braid of sweet grass and cut off 2 or 3 inches of it and burned it for perfume. (Pl. 49.) Young men braided sweet grass with their hair for the perfume. Young men wore two braids of sweet grass around their necks, the braids being joined in the back and falling on either side of the neck like braids of hair.

The birch and the cedar were regarded as " sacred " by the Chippewa. The two reasons for this " sacredness " are closely connected. One is the great usefulness of these trees to the Chippewa and the other is their connection with Winabojo, yet these two reasons are really one, for everything that is a benefit to the tribe is traced to Winabojo, the mythical character who, it is said, taught the Chippewa to live in their natural environment and yet, by his apparently witless actions, gave them an endless supply of humor. The amusing stories of Winabojo are told and retold by the old people around the winter fire. A misunderstanding of these humorous stories has given to some students an impression that Winabojo was a fantastic deity, but the old, thoughtful Indians understood him to be the source and impersonation of the lives of all sentient things, human, faunal, and floral. He endowed these sentient things with life, and taught to each its peculiar ruse for deceiving its enemies and prolonging its life. His "tricks" were chiefly exhibitions of his ability to outwit the enemies of life. He was thus regarded as the master of ruses, but he also possessed great wisdom in the prolonging of life. It was he who gave the Indians their best remedies for treating the sick, and who taught the animals the varied forms of protective disguise by which their lives can be extended. His own inherent life was so strong that, when apparently put to death, he reappeared in the same or a different form. This character, under slightly different names, appears in many Algonquian tribes, among the spellings of his name being Nanabush, Minabozho, and Nenabozho.[11]

The stories of Winabojo and the birch and cedar trees were told by Mrs. Razer, whose ceremonial felling of a birch tree is described on pages 386 and 387.

LEGEND OF WINABOJO AND THE BIRCH TREE

There was once an old woman living all alone on the shore of Lake Superior. She had a little girl living with her whom she called her daughter, though she did not know exactly where the child came from. They were very poor and the little girl went into the woods and dug wild potatoes or gathered rose berries for them to eat. The little girl grew up to be a woman, but she kept on doing the same work, getting potatoes and berries and picking up fish that were

[11] See Handbook of American Indians, Bull. 30, Bur. Amer. Ethn., pt. 2, pp. 19–23.

washed ashore. One day when doing this she had a strange feeling as though the wind were blowing underneath her clothing. She looked around her but saw no signs of anyone. After a while she went home.

As soon as she entered the house her mother saw that she looked troubled and bewildered. Her mother asked, "Did you see anyone? Did anyone speak to you?" The girl replied, "I saw no one and heard no one speak to me." After a time the mother noticed that the girl was pregnant and questioned her again but the girl replied as before, that she had seen no one. The only thing strange to her was the sensation of the wind blowing about her which she had described to her mother. When the time came for her to be delivered there was a sound as of an explosion and the girl disappeared, leaving absolutely no trace. The old woman threw herself on the ground and wailed because her daughter had disappeared. She searched everywhere but could find no trace of her. Finally, in looking among the leaves, she saw a drop of blood on a leaf. She picked it up carefully and put it beside her pillow. After a while, as she lay there, she thought she heard some one shivering and breathing near her head. She lay still, not knowing what to do. She heard the breathing near her head constantly. As she lay there wondering what it could be she heard a sound like that of a human being. She said, "I guess I am going to be blessed." [12] As she lay there a voice spoke and said, "Grandmother, get up and build a fire. I am freezing." The old woman arose and looked around, and there beside her lay a little boy. She took him up and caressed him. She got up and made a fire to warm him, and behold the child was Winabojo. All the spirits that roam the earth were frightened at the birth of Winabojo, for they knew his power. Throughout his human life he was a mysterious being with miraculous powers. He grew rapidly in strength and soon began to help his grandmother. He dug potatoes and brought fish and berries for her.

One day, when he had grown to be almost a man, he asked his grandmother what was the largest fish in the lake. She replied, "Why do you ask? It is not good for you to know. There is a large fish that lives over by that ledge of rock, but it is very powerful and would do great harm to you." Winabojo asked, "Could the great fish be killed?" His grandmother replied, "No; for he lives below the rocks and no one could get down there to kill him."

Winabojo began to think about this and he made up his mind that he would learn to fight so that he could kill the great fish. He got some wood and began to make bows and arrows. Then he asked his

---

[12] This phrase is commonly used to designate a supernatural visitation or other direct evidence of supernatural favor.

grandmother if she knew of any bird whose feathers he could put on the arrows to make them effective. The old woman replied "No The only bird whose feathers would make the arrows effective is a bird that lives in the sky, at the opening of the clouds. One would have to go up there to get the feathers." Winabojo began to think how he could go up there and get the feathers that he was determined to have. At lást he said to himself, "There is a high cliff on the edge of the lake. I will go up there and stay a while."

When he reached the high cliff he wished that he might change into a little rabbit. So he became a little rabbit and lived there. One day he went on a very high part of the cliff and called to a big bird, saying, "Eagle, come here. I am a cunning little animal. I would be a nice plaything for your children." The bird flew down and saw the little rabbit playing there. The rabbit was the cunningest thing he had ever seen. The big bird was the thunderbird and he alighted on the top of the high cliff, near the little rabbit. Finally he took the little rabbit and flew up, up toward the opening in the sky.

When the thunderbird came to his nest he called to his children, "I have brought you something very cunning to play with." His wife spoke to him very crossly and said, "Why did you bring that rabbit up here? Have you not heard that Winabojo is on the earth? There is no knowing what you have picked up." But the little rabbit was very meek and quiet, letting the children play with him as they liked. The big birds were seldom at home as they went away to get food for their children.

All at once, one day, Winabojo began to talk to himself and he said, "These children throw me around as though I was nothing. Don't they know I came here to get some of their feathers?" The next time the old birds went away he changed into his human form, took a club, killed the little thunderbirds and pulled off their feathers. He hurried around and tied the feathers up in bundles for he was sure the old birds would soon be home. When all was ready he jumped off. He was not killed because he was a *manido* (spirit) and nothing could hurt him. He was unconscious for a time after he fell on the earth but he was not hurt. Soon there was a great roaring in the sky with flashes of lightning. The thunderbirds were coming after him. Winabojo jumped up when he saw the flashes of lightning and heard the thunder. The lightning was the flash of the thunderbirds' eyes and the roaring was their terrible voices. He snatched up the bundles of feathers and ran for his life. Wherever he went the flashes and the roaring followed him, but he held on to the feathers. He had gotten what he wanted and he did not intend to lose them. The thunderbirds kept after him and at last he felt that they were tiring him out. He began to fear that he would be killed after all. The thunderbirds came so close that they almost grasped him with their claws. He was getting bewildered. They were almost upon him when he saw an old, fallen birch tree that was hollow. He crept into the hollow just in time to save his life. As he got in the thunderbirds almost had their claws on him.

The thunderbirds said, " Winabojo, you have chosen the right protection. You have fled to a king-child." There they stopped. They could not touch him for the birch tree was their own child and he had fled to it for protection. There he lay while the thunder rolled away and the flashes of the thunderbirds' eyes grew less bright. He was safe.

When the thunderbirds had gone away Winabojo came out of the hollow birch tree and said, "As long as the world stands this tree will be a protection and benefit to the human race. If they want to preserve anything they must wrap it in birch bark and it will not decay. The bark of this tree will be useful in many ways, and when people want to take the bark from the tree they must offer tobacco to express their gratitude." So Winabojo blessed the birch tree to the good of the human race. Then he went home, fixed his arrows with the feathers of the little thunderbirds and killed the great fish.

Because of all this a birch tree is never struck by lightning and people can safely stand under its branches during a storm. The bark is the last part of the tree to decay, keeping its form after the wood has disintegrated, as it did in the tree that sheltered Winabojo.

The little short marks on birch bark were made by Winabojo but the " pictures " on the bark are pictures of little thunderbirds. (Pl. 52, b.) It was said that the bark in some localities contains more distinct pictures of the little thunderbirds than in others.[13]

LEGEND OF WINABOJO AND THE CEDAR TREE

Many generations ago after Winabojo disappeared from the earth he lived on an island toward the sunrise. The direction of the sunset indicates death, but Winabojo was still alive and he lived in the east toward the sunrise. He could not be destroyed because he was *manido*, neither could he be permitted to roam at will as he had done, so he was placed on this island to stay there as long as the earth endures.

At that time there was a man who had only one daughter and she died. He felt that he could not live without her and kept telling his friends that he wanted to go to the spirit land and get his daughter.

---

[13] A collection of stories regarding this hero may be found in Jones's Ojibwa Texts, ed. Truman Michelson, vol. VII, Publications of the American Ethnological Society. The works of Schoolcraft, Radin, De Jong, Skinner, and George E. Laidlaw should be mentioned in this connection.

He was told that if he could find Winabojo he would learn the way
to the spirit land, for Winabojo was the only one who could tell him.
So he talked it over with the other Grand Medicine man, and five of
them said they would go to the spirit land with him if they could
first find the way to Winabojo. They went to the graves of their
friends and called to their spirits. Finally they got a response.
They asked, " Can we find Winabojo? " And the spirits of their
friends answered, " Yes, for he is still on the earth." Then the
spirits told them how to find him. They went until they came to
this island, far in the great lake (Superior). There they found
Winabojo. He was too old to travel, and on his head was a beautiful
cedar tree. Winabojo wore the cedar tree as an ornament and its
roots were all around him. Beside him was a great round stone.
One of the men asked if he could live always, as Winabojo was
doing. Winabojo replied, " No. You can only live your allotted
years. The only way you can become perpetual is by becoming a
stone." The man said, " Yes. I will do so." Then the man became
a stone and remained with Winabojo. The others wanted to go to
the spirit land. Winabojo gave each of them a " snake chain "[13a] and
told them to be sure not to untie these chains from around their
waists. He said, " You must stay only four days and four nights.
You will not see the spirits by day, but at night they have a dance
in the long wigwam.[14] Go in quietly and sit down." To the father
he said, " Your daughter is there. Watch for her at the dance of the
spirits in the long wigwam. Perhaps she will come and you will see
her. Carry a bag with you. Put her in the bag and hold her tight.
This is the only way in which you can get her."

The Grand Medicine men did as Winabojo told them to do. There
were only five remaining, as one had been turned into a stone. They
went to the land of the spirits and sat quietly, watching the dance of
the spirits in the long wigwam. All went well until the second day
when one of the men wanted to untie his " snake chain " and see
what would happen. He did this, and in a moment he became a
spirit and his friends never saw him again. The remaining four
men went to the dance every night and the father watched for his
daughter. On the fourth night toward morning he saw her come
into the wigwam. Her head was covered by her blanket but he
recognized her, and when she came near he grasped her in his arms.
She struggled, but by the help of his friends he got her into the bag.
Then they all returned to Winabojo, and he told them how they could
get her back to the earth. He told them to start on their way, and
when night came they were to tie the bag in a safe place, then retrace

---

[13a] This is a plaited chain worn as a protection against reptiles or other harm.
[14] This refers to the long dome-roofed structure in which the Midewiwin held its meet-
ings. Cf. beliefs concerning the northern lights, p. 379.

their steps as far as a person's voice could be heard and make their
camp.   They were told to do this every night until they reached home.
They did as Winabojo had instructed them and reached home safely.
Winabojo had told them to make a sweat lodge and they made it.
He also said there must be no crying nor wailing.   Inside the sweat
lodge he made a bed of cedar boughs and on it he laid the bag that he
had brought from the spirit land.   He did everything as Winabojo
had commanded and sat down outside the lodge.   After a while he
heard his daughter say, " Come and let me out."   He went into the
lodge, untied the bag, and his daughter came out.   He greeted her,
but there was no outcry, as Winabojo had commanded.   Then his
daughter was the same as before she went to the spirit land.

GATHERING BIRCH BARK AND CEDAR BARK

It was customary to gather as much bark as possible in June or
early in July as the bark is more easily removed at that season.
The gathering of birch and cedar bark was attended with a simple
ceremony, as both these trees are believed to be connected with Winabojo.   The foregoing legends concerning these trees have stated that
the birch is so powerful that Winabojo went to it for protection, and
the cedar is so beautiful that he wears it as an ornament.   Many sorts
of birch bark were cut, the heaviest being used for canoes or similar
purposes, and the lighter for utensils and various containers, or for
roof coverings.   Cedar was needed for parts of canoes and for numerous other uses.   In old times the procuring of birch and cedar bark
was an event in which all participated.   A number of families went
to the vicinity of these trees and made a camp.   A gathering was held,
at which a venerable man, speaking for the entire company, expressed
gratitude to the spirit of the trees and of the woods, saying they had
come to gather a supply which they needed, and asking permission
to do this together with protection and strength for their work.
He also asked the protection and good will of the thunderbirds so
that no harm would come from them.   The reason he asked the
protection of the spirit of the woods was that sometimes people
were careless and cut trees thoughtlessly, and the trees fell and hurt
them.   The speaker then offered tobacco to the cardinal points, the
sky, and the earth, murmuring petitions as he did so.   He then put
the tobacco in the ground at the foot of the tree.   Filling a pipe, he
offered it as he had offered the tobacco, again murmuring petitions.
He then lit and smoked the pipe while tobacco was distributed among
the company, who smoked for a time.   This simple ceremony was
followed by a feast.   The next day the company divided into small
groups and proceeded to cut the trees and remove the bark.

In order to observe the felling of a birch tree the writer asked
Mrs. Razer to cut down a tree.   This she and her husband consented

to do. Mrs. Razer habitually follows the old custom of placing tobacco in the ground when gathering any of the products of nature, so the old ceremony was performed in all sincerity. Considerable care was bestowed on the selection of a suitable tree, and one was at last found in the center of a large grove. It was a straight tree with smooth bark, and, after felling, was found to be 38 feet long, 27 inches in circumference next the ground, and 18 inches in circumference at the top of the stump. Birch trees grow slowly, and it was said this tree was probably 25 years old. Mrs. Razer offered tobacco to the cardinal points and the zenith, murmuring petitions, and buried it at the foot of the tree. She then wielded the ax and cut the tree, the cut being 28 inches above the ground, after which her husband completed the felling. It is the rule that all the chopping of a birch tree shall be on one side so that the tree after felling will rest on the stump. This prevents the bark being soiled by falling on the ground.

In removing the bark a vertical cut is made, the bark is turned back with the left hand, passed under the trunk of the tree and removed by the right hand. (Pl. 53, *a*, *b*.) The width of the strips depends on the intended use of the bark. An average width is about 24 inches. The uppermost branches of a tree are observed with special care as the bark on the upper branches is often clear and smooth, though the trunk of the tree has been scarred, or has had its bark removed at some previous time. The tree is permitted to remain as it falls, and when thoroughly dry is used for fuel.

Utensils are often made as soon as a tree is cut. (Pl. 53, *c*.) The sheets of bark for future use are tied in thick packs by means of strips of freshly cut basswood trees that usually grow among the birches. One hundred sheets usually constitute one of these packs. A pack is carried on a woman's back by a strap. (Pl. 48, *b*). This is stored at her home in the village, a larger supply being in a birch-bark storehouse at her maple sugar camp. The uses of birch bark are many and various.

In the southern part of the White Earth Reservation the writer witnessed the offering and burying of tobacco by a medicine man who wished to cut pine bark for medicinal use. The remedy was his own and he described several instances of its successful use.

ARTICLES MADE OF BIRCH BARK

Before entering upon a partial enumeration of articles made of birch bark it seems fitting to note some of the properties of this substance, which formed so large a factor in the economic life of the Chippewa. First, and most important, is its varied thickness.

The heaviest bark, from large trees, comprises six to nine distinct layers and is so strong that it could be made into canoes carrying many persons. The thinnest birch bark is like tissue paper but so tough that it was used in wrapping small packets tied with a thin strand of basswood fiber. (Pl. 43, *b*.) Between these extremes were many grades of thickness into which the bark of moderate sized trees could be split. A proficient woman worker could usually obtain the quality she desired either from her supply in storage or by felling a tree of suitable size. A peculiarity of birch bark is that it keeps from decay whatever is stored in it. Edibles were stored in makuks, even a gummy maple sirup being safely stored for a year in this manner. Heavy birch bark was wrapped around the bodies of the dead. Two contradictory qualities are interesting to observe. The bark was highly inflammable, being used as tinder and for torches, and yet it was possible to use freshly cut bark as a cooking utensil, the inner surface being exposed to the fire.

Birch bark was commonly available and was used for hastily made containers of various sorts. Thus a person gathering spruce gum or a few berries would cut a piece of birch bark, fold it into a "scoop" and use it temporarily. If birch bark articles split they were mended with balsam gum. With this care a makuk or tray might be used for 10 years.

It was said that when a woman was cutting birch bark she often "sharpened her knife" by drawing it across her hair.

Birch bark can be unrolled only by exposing it to the heat of a fire. When heated it becomes pliable, and retains any form in which it is placed when thus softened.

Makuks.—These were of various sorts, according to their use. The most common makuk was that used for storing maple sugar. (Pl. 34.) These makuks were sewed with split roots, and had a thin piece of basswood bark around the top, sewed over and over with split roots, like the top of a canoe. They ranged in size from makuks holding about 1 pound of sugar to those holding 20 or 30 pounds. A cover with slanting sides was sewed over the top. A similar makuk of medium or rather large size was used as a bucket, the seams being covered with pitch and a handle attached.

The makuks used for gathering and storing berries had straight sides, and the storage makuks were frequently made with the rough outer surface of the bark on the outside. A berry gathering makuk had a loop of fiber attached to one side so it could be hung from a woman's belt as she worked. (Pl. 32, *b*.) These small makuks for gathering fruit held about a quart, and the storage makuks or those for carrying the berries frequently held 12 quarts or more. The storage makuks had no binding around the top, and were frequently made with one side higher than the other so it could be lapped over and tied. This sort of makuk was used for storing fish, over which maple sugar was sprinkled. This preserved the dried berries or fish, and it was easier to get at the contents in this type of makuk than in the sort used for maple sugar.

Funnels or cones.—These varied in size from the tiny cones filled with hard sugar and hung on a baby's cradle board and the somewhat larger cones similarly filled for the delectation of children to the large funnels made of heavy bark and sewed with split roots that were used chiefly for pouring hot fat into bladders for storage. Spoons made of bark were also used. (Pl. 32, *c*.)

Dishes and trays.—For temporary and household use the birch-bark dishes were not always stiffened and bound at the top. The dishes for common use were made of birch bark folded and fastened with one or two stitches at each end. (Pl. 32, *b*, at right-hand end.) These were tied in bunches of 10 for packing or storage. The common size was about 10 inches long and 5 inches deep, though smaller and larger ones were frequently made. The shallow trays are more often seen with better finish, the superfluous bark being cut away at the ends, the overlapping edges sewed with split roots and the top finished with a stiff piece of bark, firmly sewed in place. Slippery elm bark was sometimes chewed and applied like gum to the inside of the seams on birch-bark containers to make them watertight. The largest trays were those used for winnowing wild rice. Somewhat smaller trays were used for various household purposes, including the carrying of coils of basswood fiber for making into twine. An old and rarely seen form of birch-bark dish was round, about 9 inches in diameter and 3 inches deep. The bark was adjusted in folds around the sides and the dish or tray was finished at the upper edge with two rows of sweet grass.

Cooking utensils.—It was possible to make a cooking utensil from green bark in which meat could be cooked. A Canadian Chippewa said that he had done this himself, making the container with either side of the bark outward. He said that he filled it with water and "put it right on the fire," that the part above the water might burn but the part below the water would last so long that the meat would be cooked. He said that he had heard of the putting of hot stones in the water in such a dish to heat the water, but he had not done this himself.

Coverings for dwellings.—Sheets of bark were sewn together with basswood fiber (not twisted) and made into the "birch-bark rolls" used as covers for dwellings, the sheets of bark being placed horizontally. Sticks across the ends of the roll kept it from tearing. These rolls were used most frequently on the tops of the wigwams, or lodges with frames of bent poles, but were also used on the conical tipis, and sometimes on the roof of the lodge in which maple sugar was made, this lodge having a frame like that of a house.

Meat bag.—This was commonly made of birch bark covered with soft tanned leather (pl. 54), but was also made of rawhide. It was carried on a pack strap and was used for carrying dried meat or other provisions needed on a journey. It was customary to open the bag and allow the flap to become a sort of table, from which the fragments of food were easily returned to the bag, a custom which illustrates the lack of wastefulness among these people.

Fans.—These were made in the woods whenever needed, two pieces of bark being sewed together and slipped into a cleft stick, which served as a handle. (Pl. 55, *b*.) A man might carry a fan ornamented with feathers, one specimen having the bark cut off squarely and a row of stiff feathers forming the upper portion of the fan. (Pl. 55, *c*.) Plate 55, *a*, shows an owl-feather fan with handle of birch bark. A woman never used an ornamented fan.

Torches and tinder.—Various forms of torches were made by twisting birch bark into cylinders, some of which would last an entire night, and were used by travellers. Slender torches, which could be stuck on the end of a stick that was upright in the ground, were used by women when working around the camp. A woman kept a supply of scraps of thin birch bark for use in kindling fires.

Figures.—A variety of figures were cut from birch bark. (Pls. 52, *c;* 56.) Some appear to have been for pleasure, while others represent dream symbols and totem marks (clan symbols).

Patterns.—Every woman who did beadwork had patterns cut from stiff birch bark which she laid on the material to be decorated. Mrs. English said that she remembered when patterns were pricked with a stiff fishbone around the outline and then cut with scissors. In this way the pattern was evident to the eye before the cutting was begun. With very few exceptions the cut patterns collected by the writer show no trace of a marking implement, the appearance being that the patterns are cut without tracing. (Pl. 57.)

Transparencies.—The most primitive form of Chippewa art is that in which the only material is a broad leaf or thin piece of birch bark and the only tools are human teeth and deft fingers. The leaf or birch bark is folded and indented with the teeth, this process being repeated according to the elaborateness of the design. The result is a transparency, the surface of the leaf or bark forming the background and the tooth marks forming the pattern. The native word for this is composed of two words, one meaning picture, and the other *he bites*, or *gnaws*. The leaf and bark are not wholly opaque and the tooth marks do not cut entirely through them, so the finished work shows a heavier and a lighter density of material which is

a, CUTTING BIRCH BARK PREPARATORY TO REMOVING

b, REMOVING BIRCH BARK FROM TREE

c, MAKING CONTAINER FROM BIRCH BARK

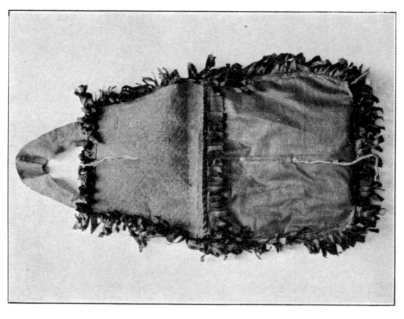

MEAT BAG, OPEN AND CLOSED

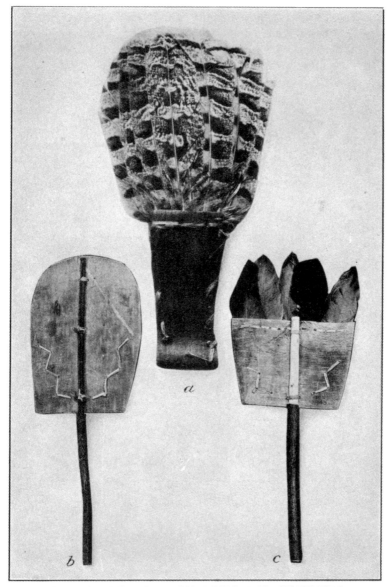

FANS MADE OF BIRCH BARK AND FEATHERS

FIGURES CUT FROM BIRCH BARK

PATTERNS CUT FROM BIRCH BARK

LEAVES IN WHICH PATTERNS HAVE BEEN BITTEN

soft and pleasing to the eye. The teeth used in making the impression were the eyeteeth and "side teeth," the folded material being indented in a variety of ways, ranging from a sharp prick, like the prick of an awl, to a broad mark produced by slightly twisting the bark between the teeth. More than 200 birch-bark transparencies have been collected by the writer, and some of the best patterns were made by a woman who had only one upper tooth. The bark used was the soft, fine inner layers of the white birch, and it was slightly warmed to render it more pliable.

The origin of this art is obscure, but it seems probable that it arose in a somewhat casual manner. A woman seated on the ground or in the wigwam might take a broad leaf or bit of thin birch bark, fold it, bite a few lines in it, unfold it and hold it up to look at it. As the result was pleasurable she might seek to improve upon her first work and others might seek to copy or emulate it. Leaves best adapted to the purpose would be selected, it would naturally be found that the birch bark could be folded and indented better if it was first warmed before the fire, and gradually a more elaborate folding of the bark would produce more interesting patterns. The information obtained from aged members of the tribe and the specimens of the art which they have been able to execute give no evidence of the influence of the white race nor of any connection with textile or ceramic art except that some of the patterns were copied in beadwork. It had no connection with a ceremony, and no symbolism, except that dream symbols might be indented and used as patterns for beadwork in the same manner that the symbol of a man's dream might be outlined in paint. It was an art with a recognized technique, producing results of a wide variety in the form of articles that were kept, exchanged, and compared, and in which the workers felt a personal pride. It was peculiar to the Algoquian tribes and was a phase of the tribal life that has passed away, and with the passing of that life the art has become almost extinct. It formed a pastime of the winter evenings, when the young people were seated in the wigwam with no other light than the fire, and it was especially practiced during the sugar camp, in early spring, when there was an abundance of birch bark at hand, and it was softer than later in the season, thus being better adapted to the making of transparencies. A few women of the younger generation (30 to 40 years of age) can indent the bark, but their patterns, as will be shown, have lost the artistic value of the earlier period.

The art had two branches, one of which appears to have been an outgrowth of the other and to have been practiced less extensively. The principal, and apparently the first, phase of the art was intended chiefly for pleasure and had a secondary use in suggesting patterns for woven beadwork. In this phase the indentations were of varying sorts, producing an agreeable art object. The patterns that appear in such transparencies are geometrical and conventional, but include life forms and some representations of tipis and houses. Such are the "pictures" that were admired, kept, or exchanged among members of the tribe. Those intended as suggestions for patterns in woven beadwork were purposely adapted for their special use as knee bands, headbands, etc. The second branch of the art is clearly related to the period in which the delicacy of the old perception was passing away. (See p. 395.) Thicker bark was used, the outline of a leaf or flower was sharply indented and the pattern cut out, after which it was fastened to cloth and outlined in beads. Mrs. Julia Warren Spears, 89 years of age, said that she saw the Chippewa girls using these patterns for beadwork when she was matron of the school at Leech Lake, about the year 1865. At that period the present floral patterns were either coming into use or were at a height of popularity, and the rather clumsy patterns made of bitten bark may in part account for the lack of artistic value in these patterns. Mrs. Spears said that they "took a leaf or flower to go by" when biting the pattern, which marks it clearly as belonging to the imitative, not the interpretative, period of culture. The influence of Government schools had taken the place of that admiration of nature and appreciation of its mysteries which underlies all effort at interpretation. The Chippewa were being taught to become copyists, and the essentials of art were lost forever.

Only two mentions of this art have been found in writings on the subject. The earliest refers to the old form and the later to the modern appl cation of the art. Schoolcraft states that "amongst the Ch ppewas of Lake Superior there exists a very ingenious art of dental pictography, or a mode of biting figures on the soft and fine inner layers of the bark of the betula papyracea, specimens of which are herewith exhibited. This pretty art appears to be confined chiefly to young females. The designs presented are imitations of flowers, fancy baskets, and human figures. There are so many abatements to the amenities of social life in the forest that it is pleasing to detect the first dawnings of the imitative and aesthetic arts."[15] This paragraph is accompanied by an illustration " from the originals," with the title " Chippewa toothwork, dental pictorial figures on the inner bark of the Betula papyracea." The reproduction by drawing and engraving does not represent the method with any degree of accuracy, but the work itself is clearly the same as that described to the writer and illustrated in Plates 58–63.

---

[15] Schoolcraft, Henry Rowe. History of the Indian Tribes in the United States, vol. 6, p. 631. Philadelphia, 1857.

The modern application of the art is mentioned by Speck, who says that among the Montagnais "the patterns for decorating birch bark consist of thin paper-bark stencils made by folding and biting designs in them with the teeth." Also, "The bitten paper-bark copy patterns supply practically all of the motives of these people." [16]

The Mille Lac Chippewa made little or no mention of the biting of patterns in a broad leaf, but Mrs. English said she remembered seeing it done by the Chippewa at La Pointe, on Lake Superior, and the writer was informed that it was commonly done on the Manitou Rapids Reserve in Ontario. A specimen of the leaf was obtained there, and was identified as *Clintonia borealis*. This leaf with a simple pattern bitten in it is shown in Plate 58.

The technique of biting birch bark is impossible to describe beyond the statement that the bark is placed between the upper and lower teeth, usually the eyeteeth, and that the teeth are brought together, either sharply or with a slightly grinding motion. One informant said that the bark was slightly twisted between the teeth. The simplest technique is shown in the patterns used for beginners in beadwork, the intention being to use one bead for each prick. The manner of folding and refolding the bark is also an important part of the technique. The pattern is in the mind of the worker and she does not hesitate or unfold the bark during the process of biting the pattern. In reply to an inquiry, a woman said that when she unfolded the bark she found the design to be what she expected because she "had the pattern in her mind before she began to bite it." One transparency is never copied from another, but an attempt to vary a pattern is suggested by Plate 59, *a* and *k*, made by the same woman. In one pattern it was found that 24 thicknesses of bark had been indented at the same time, yet the pattern was clear and the marks were uniform. It was not unusual for 12 thicknesses of bark to be indented at the same time.

The range of subjects is wide and includes geometric designs, flowers, leaves, and stars, men and women, tipis and houses, animals and insects. The vegetable and life forms are natural and also conventionalized. The patterns comprise borders or "running patterns," and units based upon the circle, square, pentagon, hexagon, and octagon, and the trefoil and quatrefoil. The simplest patterns require only one folding of the bark, after which a pattern is indented along this fold. These are what may be termed "running patterns." An example of such a pattern is Plate 59, *c*. A strip of bark is folded across and the fold placed between the teeth, the pattern being "bitten" along the fold. When the bark is unfolded the pattern is

[16] Speck, Frank G. The Double-curve Motive in Northeastern Algonkian Art. Department of Mines, Memoir 42, No. 1, Anthropological Series, pp. 11, 12. Ottawa, Government Printing Office, 1914.

seen, its opposite sides, of course, being alike. Other patterns produced by one folding of the bark are Plates 59, *d*, *g*; 61, *b*, *h*; 62, *g*. Sometimes a " running pattern " was made by folding the bark twice, one fold being crosswise and the other the length of the strip. Examples of such patterns are Plate 62, *i* and *k*. More elaborate patterns of this sort were made by folding the strip of bark crosswise and also diagonally, producing such patterns as Plates 61, *f*, and 62, *f*. Such patterns as these were copied in long strips of beadwork used as chains for the neck or as narrow headbands. The manner of folding the bark for patterns Plate 59, *e*, *h*, and *l* is clearly shown. Several units were indented at the same time, forming a sort of " running pattern," but without an actual connection between the units. The most elaborate pattern of this type is Plate 61, *c*, in which five figures were indented at the same time, representing a row of dancers.

The Indians seemed to prefer to indent two units at a time, in the simpler unit patterns, while the larger and more elaborate unit patterns were indented singly, thus securing fineness of detail. The patterns shown in Plates 60, *c*, *f*, and *g*, and 62, *c*, were made double; that is, two units were indented at the same time, the photograph showing the clearer of the two. Distinct from these were the patterns made singly which required several foldings and refoldings of the bark. Such patterns were regarded somewhat as an artist regards his sketches. They were exhibited and compared, and even exchanged among persons proficient in this craft.

Patterns which require only folds that are equally spaced and radiate from a common center are Plates 59, *a*, *b*, *f*, *i*, *k*; 60, *a*, *e*; and 61, *g*, *k*. Such a pattern may be inclosed in a line which is folded and indented after the rest of the pattern is finished, as in Plate 60, *b* and *k*. A close inspection of the specimen shown in Plate 60, *d*, suggests that the border was indented with the rest of the pattern. The folding in Plate 60, *h*, is shown in detail and includes a diagonal fold intersecting the diagonals that radiate from the center. A pentagonal form is shown in Plate 60, *i*. A somewhat complicated folding was required for Plate 60, *e*, the bark being folded crosswise, lengthwise, and diagonally, the pattern being smoothed out between the several foldings and then creased for the next part of the design. In Plate 61, *a*, we find a crease with indentations along only a part of its length, beyond which the line divides into two diagonals. These lines form the framework of the pattern, like the stems of a cluster of flowers, which, with leaves, are produced by additional foldings of the bark. The pattern appears to represent two conventionalized flowers, with leaves below them. This pattern was made at White Earth. The design Plate 62, *a*, bears a resemblance to it, and was made on the Manitou Rapids

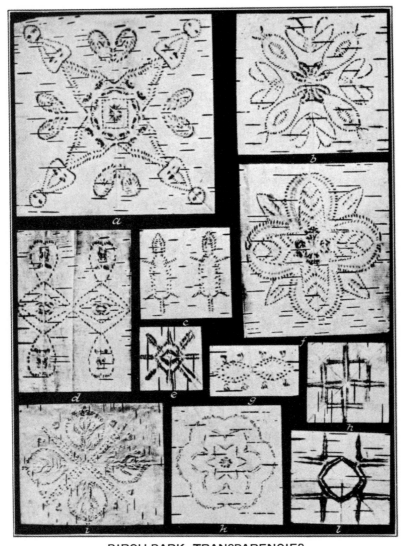

BIRCH-BARK TRANSPARENCIES

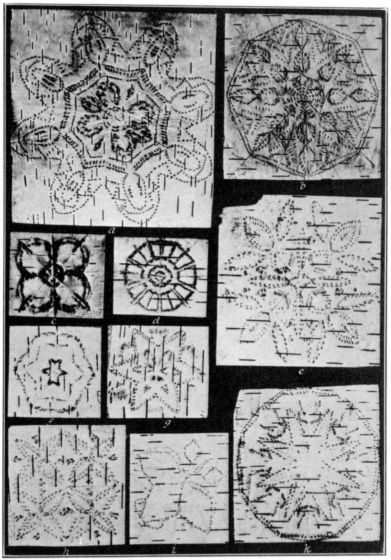

BIRCH-BARK TRANSPARENCIES

BIRCH-BARK TRANSPARENCIES

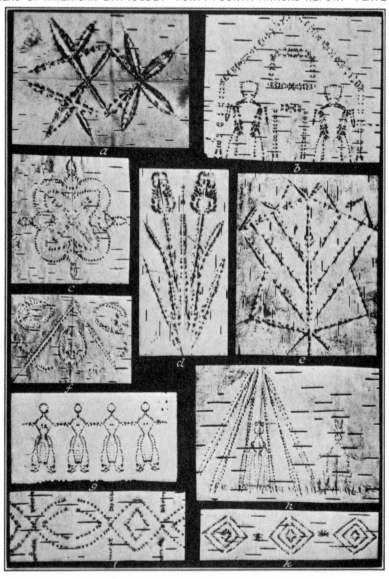

BIRCH-BARK TRANSPARENCIES

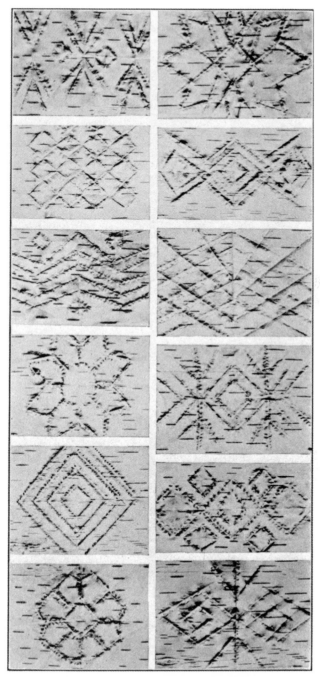

BIRCH-BARK TRANSPARENCIES

Reserve in Canada. Other interesting designs from that reserve are Plate 62, *d* and *e*, the former showing curved lines (or creases) which are unusual in birch-bark transparencies. The bark available by the Canadian Chippewa women was too stiff and heavy for delicate work. The season was July, and the bark is less pliable than in early spring if freshly gathered, and the Canadian women had not stored so generous a supply of bark as the Minnesota Chippewa. As already noted, the bark needed for use during the summer was gathered in the spring and stored in a dark, cool shed, which preserved its soft texture, and this storage of bark was being carried on by the women at White Earth when the present research was in progress. The pattern Plate 62, *e*, is different from any collected in Minnesota and required twelve foldings for its production.

Both straight and diagonal folds were required for the patterns Plate 62, *b* and *h*, the latter showing the features of the woman in the tipi with as much clearness as those of the dancer in Plate 61, *c*. Attention is directed to the difference in the shape of the faces in these two patterns, also to the variety in the markings on Plate 62, *b*, showing a distinct technique. These are from White Earth.

The patterns here illustrated were selected from a collection of more than 200, obtained from the older women at White Earth and Red Lake in Minnesota, and the Manitou Rapids Reserve in Canada. The decline of this interesting craft is seen in the work of Indian women of the younger generation, one example being shown as Plate 61, *d*. It will be noted that the outlines are blurred by a process that approaches a nibbling of the bark, while the design lacks the grace and repose of the older examples. The clear thinking of the old days has passed away, and in its place has come a belief that by doing a thing uncertainly, over and over, one can accomplish as good results as by a carefully planned, definite procedure.

The designs shown in Plate 63 were made on the Manitou Rapids Reserve in Ontario, Canada, and show a somewhat different type than those in the previous illustrations. As stated, they were made when the bark was rather heavy, which can be seen in the texture of the pieces. The creases are more apparent and the marks less sharp than in thinner bark. Some of the designs would form " running patterns " while others are single units which could readily be placed side by side to form extended decorations.

The following story is related concerning the custom of making birch-bark transparencies:

There was once a man who lived with his parents. At sugar-making time he noticed that they were getting old and the work was hard for them, so he brought home a wife to help them. The family were in the sugar camp and he sent his wife to get some birch bark for making dishes as the other women did. She took an ax and was gone all day. When she came home at night she had a great bundle of bark on her back. This made him glad, for he thought she had been very industrious. She opened her bundle and said, " See what I have been doing all day." Then she showed him quantities of patterns and pictures bitten in birch bark. Her bundle was full of them. She had been biting patterns all day instead of making dishes.

The man was so ashamed that he hung his head and died. He could not bear to have people know that he had brought home such a good-for-nothing wife.

Etching and self-patterns on birch bark.—Bark taken from birches in the early spring has the tender " sap-bark " of the previous year next to the outer bark. If the bark gathered at this time is put in hot water the " sap-bark " turns dark brown while the outer layers of bark remain light in color. This renders possible a wide variety of decoration in contrasting colors. Dishes are made with this dark color as a foundation and the decoration is supplied with a sharp implement, the lines showing the light color of the under layer of bark and the contrast remaining after the bark has dried. The implement used for this purpose was a pointed stick or the " splint-bone " from the heel of a deer, preferably a young doe. The bark is in the right stage for this work at the season of sugar making, and many sugar makuks are made with the dark surface of the bark on the outside, etched with simple decorations. A typical example is the sugar makuk in Plate 34, which is etched with parallel horizontal lines between which are vertical, diagonal, or zigzag lines arranged in simple groupings. The fresh sugar was often stored in them and used as a gift, the decoration making the gift more attractive. At the present time this work is frequently done in a freehand drawing of leaves and flowers, the designs being without artistic value.

Another type of decoration made possible by the condition of the bark at this season may be called " self-patterns " in birch bark. Sometimes the pattern appears in the light color on a dark background and sometimes the colors are reversed, the design being in the light shade. In a typical example of this work a rather large, conventional pattern cut from birch bark or paper is laid on the bark and a line is drawn around it. This is still done at Grand Portage, where old methods of work are continued. The design is etched on the inner surface of the freshly cut bark, cutting through the " sap-bark," after which, if desired, the work may be laid aside. When it is to be finished the bark is moistened with hot water, and on the portion which is to be in light color the thin tissue of bark is removed in small particles or shreds with a sharp knife. Thus if the makuk is to be dark in color with light-colored leaves the surface within the etching of the leaves is carefully removed. If the colors are to be reversed it is necessary to remove all the surface except that within the etching. As indicated, if the makuk is to be filled with fresh sugar it is finished at the camp, but if the article is to be for some general purpose, the woman does the part of the work which must be done while the bark is fresh and takes the article with her, to finish at leisure. The completion can not, however, be deferred too long or the dark surface of bark can not be removed with neatness.